THE AVOIDANT ATTACHMENT WORKBOOK

Get Over the Fear of Intimacy, Uncover Deactivation Triggers, and Move to Secure Attachment

ELIZABETH SUMMERS

TABLE OF CONTENTS

INTRODUCTION

We all have trouble with our relationships, both as teenagers and as adults. Some of this is as a result of personalities or different ways of thinking. However, the way we emotionally connect with the people in our lives is largely based on how our parents, guardians, and trusted adults interacted with us when we were children.

Mental health experts began studying relationships more than a century ago. Far more recently, John Bowlby and Mary Ainsworth began to develop what has come to be known as the Attachment theory. According to this theory, our earliest relationships determine how we learn to interact and attach to people as we become teenagers and adults.

This book examines the avoidant attachment style, how you can identify it in yourself or those who love, and how you can work to develop more secure attachments with the people in your life.

Navigating This Workbook

Each chapter is broken down into sections. Ideas, techniques, and concepts are introduced, and then you will have exercises that demonstrate how to use what you've just learned. The most effective way to use this workbook is to go through it in chronological order. Each section and chapter builds on what you learned in the previous section or chapter. The further you go into the workbook, the more knowledge you should have to understand the next important concept, tool, technique, and exercise.

You will be spending a lot of time thinking back on past experiences as part of the exercises, and this will often involve exploring your darker emotions because those are the ones that require the most work to deal with.

Make sure you are in a safe space to go through the activities.

Even things that happened years ago in your life can cause strong emotions. These events are the reason why people develop an avoidant attachment style, so intentionally thinking of them is likely to trigger some unhappy memories, if not some horrible ones.

While we aren't asking you to relive your worst and most traumatic emotional reactions, you may end up thinking about these events as you start delving into your emotions to understand them.

If you have issues or find you are having intense, negative emotional reactions, seek help from a therapist or get a medical expert to help you. People who have been through traumatic events often need professional help to learn how to control intense and almost uncontrollable emotions.

Overview of the Avoidant Attachment Style

The avoidant attachment style is often seen as problematic because people who display this particular attachment style tend to avoid getting emotionally attached to the people in their lives. They don't feel that they are able to rely on anyone except themselves, so instead of building relationships, they tend to push people away. This approach to life is often couched as the person valuing their freedom and independence too much to rely on anyone else. It hides the fact that they don't feel comfortable or confident that a relationship will last, so they don't see a relationship as being worth the effort since it will eventually fail. As a result, they are more likely to undermine or sabotage relationships, usually without realizing that is what they are doing.

There is nothing wrong with being self-reliant, but it should not come at the cost of developing healthy relationships. They tend to dislike dealing with emotions, and the more a person presses them to get close, the more likely they are to withdraw. It is easier for them to dismiss emotions, whether theirs or someone else's.

The problem is that studies have proven that people live longer, happier lives when they have healthy relationships and are able to have secure attachments to the people in their lives.

It is wrong to say that there is something wrong with people who have this attachment style, but it can be detrimental to a person's life. While it will take work, knowing that this is your attachment style means that you can start working to build the kind of deeper connections you haven't thought possible.

Chapter 1

UNDERSTANDING ATTACHMENT

We all struggle in relationships as adults. According to the Attachment Theory, for many of us, the problems stem from the way we learned to trust and connect with people when we were really young. This chapter provides a look at what the Attachment Theory is, the different types of attachments, and recognizing those different types. There are several attachment styles that can be problematic when it comes to adult relationships, but this book will focus on avoidant attachment styles.

The Concept of Attachment Styles

The Attachment Theory is relatively new, and it has been developed first by John Bowlby, and then by Mary Ainsworth. Based on their work, they saw some similar issues in relationships that seemed to be related to how the people were raised.

Children who grew up feeling safe are much more likely to have secure attachments as adults. When they are young, they learn that people are there to help them, and so there is a greater level of trust and security when interacting with other people. As adults, they are more likely to feel confident in themselves, find it easier to trust others, and they tend to handle conflict with others well. They also tend to have more success and healthier romantic relationships as they are more capable of communicating and navigating the challenges of being a good partner.

Children who grew up feeling afraid, neglected, or confused can have one of many other attachment styles that can make it more difficult to navigate relationships as adults. There are many attachment styles that reflect in a less than ideal home environment for infants and children. As adults, they tend to have more trouble processing and understanding their emotions, and they have trouble dealing with other people's emotions.

There are four types of attachment styles.

Secure Attachment

This is the kind of attachment style that is considered healthy and fosters better relationships when children become adults. If you have a secure attachment style, you will still have relationship troubles, and you may not always have the best reactions sometimes – we are all human. However, you are more likely to be properly equipped to handle relationship issues.

People with this attachment style tend to have a number of advantages as adults.

- They have higher self-confidence and tend to be comfortable in who they are in relationships, especially with romantic partners.
- They usually feel comfortable expressing how they feel, as well as realizing when they need help and then asking for it.
- They are able to feel happy for others, especially their partners.
- They are generally comfortable being around others, but they don't get anxious when their partner isn't around them.
- They are usually better able to maintain emotional balance, and when conflict arises, they tend to be better at navigating the problems. Part of this is them being less likely to hold grudges or negative feelings because they are better able to manage conflict.
- They are better able to handle disappointment and failure, learning lessons and doing better, especially in romantic relationships.

This is the best attachment style because it allows for people to have healthier relationships. A person who feels secure in their relationships will experience fewer negative emotions and are more likely to be happy with their lives as they aren't constantly second-guessing relationships or trying to avoid them entirely.

Anxious or Ambivalent Attachment

People who tend to be anxious or ambivalent in relationships are often seen as needy, too clingy, or in constant need of validation. Often, there is no amount of reassurance or care that a partner can show that will make that person feel adequate or secure in the relationship. Their anxious behavior can become a significant problem in any relationship, but it is particularly problematic in romantic partnerships.

People with this type of attachment style tend to face the following problems in their relationships.

- They desire to be in relationships, often craving the kind of closeness that they perceive in other relationships, but their inability to fully trust or rely on people makes them anxious when those people aren't present.
- For the people they really care about, people with this attachment style tend to become fixated on people who aren't present, particularly romantic partners. This may show in the form of excessive phone calls, hundreds of texts, and constantly checking in with the partner. This can quickly overwhelm their partners, resulting in those people leaving the relationship.
- They are more likely to have trouble with boundaries set by other people. Boundaries are often seen as threats to the relationship, and the person may start to feel panicked when a boundary is put in place. It can also make them feel afraid or angry. The problem is that the person who has this type of attachment will feel that a boundary means that their partner is pulling away, while their partner may feel that the person with this attachment style lacks basic respect for personal boundaries.
- They tend to base how they feel about themselves based on how they think others feel about them. If they feel that something or someone is a threat, they are much more likely to overreact, often further exacerbating the problem.
- To try to make themselves feel more comfortable, they are much more likely to manipulate situations, particularly using guilt, to control how their partner's behave. This is very common when they are feeling anxious or jealous, placing their emotional issues squarely on their partner's shoulders. This often leads to resentment.
- They require a lot of reassurance and attention to feel comfortable in a relationship.

People with this kind of attachment style are often quickly identified in relationships as being too needy or clingy, which is why their relationships tend to be shorter. It can be difficult to deal with their constant need for reassurance and use of guilt to try to get attention. It is difficult to be in close relationships because their insecurities often drive people away as they require a lot of attention just to feel comfortable in a relationship.

Disorganized or Fearful-avoidant Attachment

This type of attachment style is often present in people who were abused, neglected, or both as infants and children. Their difficulty in establishing healthy relationships is a part of the trauma they have experienced. Often, they feel that they don't deserve or can never earn love because there is something inherently flawed about them that will mean no one could actually love them. Even though this is never true, it is very difficult to get through to someone with this attachment style that they are deserving of love and happiness because of the deep-seated trauma. There is a general sense of mistrust and fear of the world that makes it difficult to feel comfortable or confident in anything they do.

People with this type of attachment style tend to face the following problems in their relationships.

- They are much more likely to have significant emotional swings because they find close relationships to be unsettling. This could be a result of feeling unsure why someone actually feels any kind of attachment to them.
- They may be more likely to be either insensitive of their partners. This means that they may seem to be controlling or untrusting, which can lead to harsher, more explosive arguments. This can lead to abusive behavior that mirrors what they experienced.
- It is more likely that they will be overly sensitive to their partners, constantly trying to please them. They are much more likely to spend a lot of time apologizing, even when they have nothing to apologize for. This often is a reflection of how they reacted to the abuse, meaning they may become more childlike or make themselves smaller.
- They are more likely to have addictions, particularly drugs and alcohol.
- They may have trouble accepting responsibility for their actions.

They exhibit insecurities in a way that can be similar to people with the anxious attachment style, but the root cause is very different. While a therapist is recommended for the other two insecure emotional styles, the disorganized attachment style should see a therapist to help them process their earlier issues. It is incredibly difficult to develop healthier relationships without first processing the earlier trauma and learning to love yourself.

Avoidant or Dismissive Attachment

This book will go into a lot more detail about this particular attachment style because it is seen as being incredibly difficult to bond with people. If you have this kind of attachment style, you are much more likely to have trouble dealing with emotions, but particularly someone else's emotions. When someone has an emotional reaction, you are more likely to shut down or push the person away. As a result, you are much less likely to form any kind of emotional attachment. Numerous studies have shown how this can be detrimental to a person's health.

Defining Avoidant Attachment

People with this attachment style often come across as cold and indifferent to the people around them. They are more likely to be thought of as psychopaths and sociopaths because of their desire to avoid dealing with other people's emotions (as well as their own). They decidedly are not psychopaths and sociopaths because they feel emotions, typically very strongly, but they are not equipped to handle or process those emotions.

If you have an avoidant attachment style, you are much more likely to prefer to push people away because you simply don't trust people. You don't feel that people mean you well, or you are sure that they will eventually disappoint you. Instead of allowing yourself to get close to people, you prefer to remain isolated and alone. You've convinced yourself that this is the only way to protect yourself from what you feel is inevitable if you get close with other people.

Often people who exhibit this type of style had parents who rejected or abandoned them, or they were constantly distracted instead of taking care of you. Because of their apparent indifference and inability to provide predictable love and care, you learn young that you can't rely on anyone. You learned to self-soothe when you were young because you knew that you wouldn't get the comfort you need. This results in a foundation of self-reliance to the near exclusion of anyone else. You find it easier to deal with the issues caused by the lack of intimacy instead of the inevitable disappointment of a relationship failing.

One of the few positives is that you are less likely to feel lonely because you do rely on yourself. However, you are more likely to do too much and to overburden yourself both professionally and personally because you don't trust people enough to delegate tasks to them.

On the surface, people who have an avoidant attachment style seem happy and can be the life of the party. They come across as having high self-esteem and an admirable independence. Much about them seems to be great, but when people try to get close, they find this to be nearly impossible. They may have an easy time getting into relationships, but those relationships don't last long, so they may have many, many exes, but they don't have much experience with a real relationship.

Exploring Attachment Styles Exercises

Add workbook tasks to help people start to identify their attachment style.

Recognizing Avoidant Behaviors

This attachment style is very different from the other types because the person who has it tends to avoid actually feeling an emotional connection. People can often see exactly what is happening, even the person with the attachment style. The problem is that the person who has an avoidant attachment style usually doesn't see it as a problem. The desire to be close to someone is not as strong as the desire to not get hurt or to feel betrayed. Their fear of intimacy far outweighs what they see as the few benefits of being in a secure relationship. It often means that they come across as cold and stoic because they do not easily share what they are thinking or feeling.

They are far less likely to seek the help of a mental health expert because they are highly uncomfortable with being vulnerable. To them, the problems aren't nearly as substantial as people may think, so they continue to struggle alone.

All of these feelings and ways of thinking often result in a particular way of acting that makes it easier to identify someone with these attachment styles. The following are 10 ways that someone who tends to avoid having any serious attachments.

1. They avoid having relationships that have any real depth to them. When people start to express emotions, they tend to shut down or leave. This can be a surprise to people they interact with because people around them may feel there is a deeper relationship, so they do not expect to be shut out when something goes wrong.

2. They are much more likely to have many short-term romantic relationships. As soon as a relationship starts to feel too serious, they tend to end it. They rarely think about other people in terms of long-term relationships.

3. They are very strict on maintaining personal boundaries and require a lot more personal space. This may come across as the person being introverted, which is very likely that they are, but there is more to it than that. While introverts can live with other people as long as they have places to be alone, someone who avoids attachment is likely to hesitate or entirely refuse to merge their lives with others. They prefer to live alone because it is simply easier.

4. They are much more likely to minimize how others feel, as well as their own feelings. If an argument or issue arises, they are much more likely to walk away to avoid conflict. While this can be healthy, especially if emotions are starting to run high, it is only healthy if people discuss the issue once the emotions settle. Someone who has an avoidant attachment style often will refuse to discuss the issue or work toward a solution, which is unhealthy.

5. They are not very good at compromising, preferring to make decisions on their own, even if it affects others. They may or may not consider the needs or wants of their partner, feeling that they are making the best decision without input from anyone else. There may be good intentions behind this, but it definitely leaves partners feeling unseen and unheard.

6. They rarely ever ask for help, and probably can't even tell when they actually need outside help . They also don't see a problem with relying solely on themselves.

7. They tend to have a pull-push dynamic with the people in their lives. In the beginning, they may be engaged and interested in the early part of a relationship, but the closer someone becomes, the more likely it is that a person will start to push them away.

8. Their difficulty in allowing themselves to feel vulnerable with others means they rarely have any real discussions about emotions They also come across as being unresponsive to the needs of others.

9. They are constantly looking for signs that someone is going to reject them. It is difficult for them to feel secure that other people are as loyal as they seem, no matter how committed someone may be to them.

10. They appear to be largely unemotional because they often suppress how they are feeling or avoid allowing themselves to feel anything intensely. They virtually always respond that they are fine when asked, even when there is good reason to believe that they aren't.

There are positives to some of these responses because it means that the person isn't likely to fly off the handle, cause a lot of drama, or actively work to make other people feel worse. However, there are a lot more downsides, with the person who is primarily hurt by this style of attachment being the person who has it.

The Psychological Impact of Avoidant Attachment on Individuals

Where all of the other types of attachment styles involve having some kind of attachment to other people, even if those attachments are unhealthy, someone who is avoidantly attached doesn't really form any kind of meaningful attachment. This is by design, whether or not the person realizes it.

Their mistrust in others means that they find it incredibly difficult to form any kind of secure attachment. The first signs of problems can lead to them simply avoiding that person or ending the relationship. This is much more likely to happen since they find it difficult to open up or discuss emotions. Both the person with this attachment style and any romantic partners they have are likely to feel dissatisfied in their relationship because the connection is surface level.

Most people want to have a better understanding of their romantic partner, and this is incredibly difficult or impossible with someone who avoids talking about emotions or thoughts. Avoiding emotional intimacy is much more likely to be taken personally, even though it decidedly isn't personal.

While someone with an avoidant attachment style may not see others as trustworthy, they are usually very self-confident, at least on the surface. They feel that they are the best person to take care of the things they need. At the same time, they are incredibly critical of themselves because of a sense that they let themselves down when they don't succeed or when they aren't successful. Despite coming across as self-confident, they often experience a lot of self-degrading thoughts. These same negative thought processes are what affect how they interact with others. It is just much easier to see this as they act in a way that makes it clear they are distrustful or uninterested in a closer relationship. People don't see the inner criticisms and self-deprecating thinking as the person does not open up about their emotions. They have a very confident front, but are rarely nearly so confident or egotistical as they appear.

People with this attachment style often do not realize it for years. Since they do not talk about how they feel with others, people aren't able to point out that this is their attachment style. Once the person *does* become aware that they have an avoidant attachment style, they are less likely to see a need to change. That means that they will continue to suffer from the negative effects from the lack of connectivity with the people around them.

Having this attachment style does not mean that someone has a mental disorder. However, this type of attachment style does often lead to anxiety disorder. People who are avoidantly attached to others may experience panic attacks or high anxiety when other people try to get close or want to be in a committed relationship. They are also much more likely to suffer from depression. These problems tend to get worse as the person ages unless they start working to change how they view and approach relationships.

Exercise: Reflect on Your Own Attachment Style Through Journal Prompts

As you've explored the concept of attachment styles, it's time to turn the lens inward and reflect on your own experiences and tendencies in relationships. This exercise is designed to help you identify and understand your own attachment style, with a focus on introspection and self-awareness. Please respond to the following prompts in the spaces provided, taking your time to think deeply about your answers. Remember, there are no right or wrong responses here—this is a space for honest self-reflection.

Prompt 1: Early Relationships

Reflect on your earliest relationships, including those with family members, caregivers, and friends. How did these relationships shape your feelings about trust and security?

Your Response:

_____

_____

_____

_____

_____

_____

_____

_____

_____

_____

Prompt 2: Recognizing Patterns

Think about your past romantic relationships or close friendships. Can you identify any recurring patterns in how you relate to others? Consider aspects like communication, trust, and handling conflict.

Your Response:

_____

_____

_____

_____

_____

Prompt 3: Emotional Availability

Consider your comfort level with emotional intimacy. How easy or difficult is it for you to share your feelings with others? Do you find yourself pulling away when others get too close, or do you seek more closeness than they seem willing to provide?

Your Response:

_____

_____

_____

_____

_____

Prompt 4: Dealing with Conflict

Reflect on how you typically handle conflict in relationships. Are you more likely to confront issues directly, avoid them, or feel overwhelmed by them? How does this impact your relationships?

Your Response:

_____

_____

_____

_____

_____

Prompt 5: Independence vs. Interdependence

Think about your balance between independence and interdependence in relationships. Do you lean more towards self-reliance to the point of pushing others away, or do you struggle to maintain a sense of self when in close relationships?

Your Response:

_____

_____

_____

_____

_____

Prompt 6: Reaction to Rejection or Disappointment

Recall a time when you faced rejection or disappointment in a relationship. How did you react? What does this tell you about your attachment style?

Your Response:

_____

_____

_____

_____

_____

Prompt 7: Self-perception and Relationships

How do you think your self-perception influences your relationships? Consider how your view of yourself might impact your expectations and behavior towards others.

Your Response:

_____

_____

_____

_____

_____

Prompt 8: Desire for Change

Considering what you've learned about different attachment styles, do you see aspects of your attachment behavior you'd like to change? If so, what are they, and why?

Your Response:

_____

_____

_____

_____

_____

Exercise: Identify Behaviors in Past Relationships That Align with Avoidant Attachment

This exercise is designed to help you delve deeper into understanding avoidant attachment patterns and recognize how they may have manifested in your past relationships. By reflecting on specific behaviors, you can gain insight into how avoidant attachment influences your interactions and relationships. Below are prompts to guide your exploration. Write your responses in the spaces provided, focusing on honesty and self-reflection to foster personal growth.

Prompt 1: Emotional Distance

Recall a situation where you maintained emotional distance from a partner or friend who was seeking closeness. What were your reasons or feelings behind this behavior?

Your Response:

_____

_____

_____

_____

_____

Prompt 2: Reaction to Vulnerability

Think about a time when someone opened up to you emotionally in a way that made you uncomfortable. How did you respond to their vulnerability?

Your Response:

_____

_____

_____

_____

_____

Prompt 3: Ending Relationships

Reflect on a past relationship that you ended. Were there moments you felt the relationship was getting too close or too intense? How did this feeling influence your decision to end the relationship?

Your Response:

_____

_____

_____

_____

_____

Prompt 4: Need for Independence

Consider your need for independence within a relationship. Have there been instances where your desire for independence caused conflict or misunderstandings? Describe one such instance.

Your Response:

_____

_____

_____

_____

_____

Prompt 5: Dealing with Conflict

Think about how you handle conflicts in relationships. Do you tend to withdraw or avoid discussing the issues? Provide an example of how you've navigated conflict in a way that might reflect avoidant attachment.

Your Response:

_____

_____

_____

_____

_____

Prompt 6: Perceptions of Partners' Needs

Reflect on a time when you felt overwhelmed or suffocated by a partner's emotional needs. How did you react to these feelings, and what actions did you take as a result?

Your Response:

_____

_____

_____

_____

_____

Prompt 7: Seeking Solitude

Identify a moment when you chose solitude or isolation over spending time with a partner or friend, especially during a period when they sought your company. Why did you make this choice?

Your Response:

_____

_____

_____

_____

_____

Prompt 8: Reluctance to Share Personal Thoughts

Think about a situation where you consciously chose not to share your thoughts, feelings, or personal matters with someone close to you. What motivated this decision, and how did it affect your relationship?

Your Response:

_____

_____

_____

_____

_____

As you work through these prompts, remember that the goal is not to critique your past actions harshly but to understand them better. Recognizing patterns is the first step towards growth and healthier future relationships.

Practical Exercise : Observe Your Reactions in Social Settings

Objective:

The goal of this exercise is to become more aware of your own behaviors and reactions in various social settings, with a focus on identifying any tendencies that align with avoidant attachment. This increased awareness can help you understand your social patterns and consider adjustments to foster more meaningful connections.

Instructions:

1. **Select Social Situations:** For the next week, put yourself in a variety of social settings. These can range from casual outings with friends, family gatherings, work meetings, or community events.
2. **Observe and Reflect:** In each setting, take a step back mentally and observe your behaviors and reactions. Pay special attention to moments where you might:
   o Withdraw from conversations or groups.
   o Feel the urge to leave early or arrive late to minimize interaction.
   o Hesitate to engage in deeper, more meaningful conversations.
   o Prefer to listen rather than share personal thoughts or feelings.
   o Notice discomfort with physical proximity or touch from others.

3. **Take Notes:** After leaving each social setting, take a moment to jot down your observations. Include specific instances of avoidant behavior, your feelings at the time, and any thoughts that might have influenced your actions.
4. **Review and Reflect:** At the end of the week, review your notes. Look for patterns in your behavior across different settings and consider what these might say about your social and attachment tendencies.

Outcome:

By actively observing and reflecting on your behavior in social situations, you can gain insights into how avoidant attachment traits may be influencing your interactions. Understanding these tendencies is the first step toward addressing them and working toward forming closer, more fulfilling relationships.

Practical Exercise : Share Your Attachment Style

Objective:

This exercise aims to open up a dialogue about attachment styles with someone close to you, such as a friend, family member, or romantic partner. Sharing and discussing your attachment style can enhance understanding, empathy, and support within your relationship.

Instructions:

1. **Choose a Participant:** Select a close friend, family member, or partner whom you trust and feel comfortable discussing personal topics with.
2. **Prepare:** Reflect on your own attachment style and how it affects your behavior and relationships. Think about specific examples or patterns you've noticed in your interactions with others, especially with the person you've chosen for this exercise.
3. **Initiate the Conversation:** Find a quiet, comfortable time and place to talk. Begin by explaining the concept of attachment styles and why you think it's an important topic.
4. **Share Your Experience:** Share your thoughts on your own attachment style, providing examples from your relationship with them. Be open about your feelings, struggles, and any desires you have for growth or change.
5. **Invite Their Perspective:** Encourage them to share their thoughts and feelings about what you've said. Ask if they've noticed these behaviors and how they feel about them. This might enhance your mutual understanding and offer insightful information.
6. **Discuss Together:** Talk about ways you can support each other in addressing any challenges related to attachment styles. Consider setting goals for how you can improve communication, increase intimacy, or better support each other's needs.

Outcome:

This exercise fosters open communication and mutual understanding about how attachment styles influence your relationship. By sharing and discussing your attachment style, you and your chosen participant can work together to strengthen your bond and support each other's emotional growth and well-being.

Chapter 2

THE ROOTS OF AVOIDANCE

For the most part, children are not born expecting to be let down or avoiding relationships. There are some personality types that do, but they are incredibly rare. Avoidant attachment style is much more common, and it is rooted in how the person was treated as an infant and child. This means that it is something that can be triggered when the person is an adult. Knowing the root cause and triggers can help you to start developing more secure attachments over time.

Examining Childhood Experiences

Unlike the other two more problematic attachment styles, parents tend to be present in the child's life. The child is rarely abused, and the neglect isn't nearly so obvious because their parents are usually there and present. Instead of acting in ways that are easily viewed as negative, the way they treat their children is more nuanced. The child's physical needs are met. The problem is that their emotional needs are often ignored or are not tended to in any meaningful way. The saying, "Children should be seen, not heard," is the type of mindset that is more likely to result in an avoidant attachment style when that child becomes an adult.

When a parent or guardian is more removed or reserved around a child, that child learns to be emotionally detached from the people who are meant to love them the most. Beyond food, drink, and a safe place to stay, children need emotional support. When this is lacking or missing, children will learn that other people cannot be relied on to meet their needs. Repeated attempts at getting emotional support, especially after a negative event (such as getting injured or being bullied), that are rejected or dismissed by their caregiver teaches the child that it is simply their responsibility to deal with their own emotions. Since they have few to no positive emotional sharing experiences, they stop looking to others for emotional support. With their efforts at emotional connection being repeatedly shut down or ignored, they don't feel there is any point in attempting to look to anyone else as they get older.

Parents and guardians who tell their children to "toughen up," "stop crying," or "calm down," are likely teaching their children that emotions should be repressed or avoided. This goes for all emotions, not just negative ones. If a child is excited about an upcoming event, and they are constantly told to "calm down," "tone it down," or "stop talking about it" instead of engaging in conversation about the topic, they are learning that emotions have no place in human interactions. Their caregivers are teaching them that even happy or positive events don't need to be celebrated and aren't a cause for others to be excited or to celebrate. They may have a muted celebration of milestones, but often emotions are largely avoided as a part of the celebration. The child is expected to act like a young adult instead of to experience the emotional highs and lows that should be a part of childhood.

Unfortunately, this is a vicious cycle, and a person who develops this kind of attachment style is at high risk of doing exactly the same thing to their children – not providing emotional support or deeper connectivity. This is perhaps the most important reason for someone to develop a more secure attachment style – they want to ensure their children receive the kind of emotional support that the person with the attachment style was denied. This is also why it's so important to recognize if this is your attachment style.

There are other situations where a child may learn to hide their emotions or to bury them. If you had a helicopter parent, a parent with an anxious attachment style, you may have learned that it was best to simply avoid showing emotions. If you let them see how you felt, they could have had an extreme reaction that made you feel incredibly uncomfortable. In these cases, you learned how to manage your interactions with your parents, largely making you responsible for their emotions, instead of getting the emotional support you deserved.

Fortunately, once you are aware that you have an avoidant attachment style, you can start to change how you interact with others.

Identifying Triggers for Deactivation

The biggest trigger for someone who tends to avoid attachments is for someone to express a desire to become closer or to enter a committed relationship. Once someone expresses the desire for a deeper, more meaningful relationship or tries to get closer, the person with this attachment style will pull away or break off the relationship entirely. While this is a predictable trigger, there are some other triggers and some more nuanced ones.

The following are some of those ways that you may react by pulling away from others if you have this particular attachment style:

- When you feel someone is texting or calling you too often, you feel that you need to put more distance between you and them.
- When someone asks about the state of your relationship or asking for a more exclusive, committed relationship.
- When people start to discuss emotions.
- When someone they know asks for comfort, whether it is having someone to listen to them vent or to help them through grief. Providing any kind of emotional support makes them uncomfortable.
- When someone becomes more demanding of your attention, even if that person has a right to expect that kind of attention, such as a child.
- Romantic gestures may make the person uncomfortable, particularly big romantic gestures that hint toward a bigger commitment.
- When they feel that someone is criticizing them, they don't usually differentiate between positive feedback and negative criticism.
- Any kind of physical contact can create extreme discomfort, but particularly unexpected contact.

Sometimes these events and actions cause the person to have a panic attack or to become incredibly uncomfortable. To prevent this kind of severe reaction, people with avoidant attachment styles tend to react in more extreme ways to deactivate that negative emotional reaction. In romantic relationships, it will often result in the person ending the relationship, and this likely will happen with very little explanation. For friends and family, the person will put distance between them, sometimes going noncontact until they feel more comfortable.

Ironically, having someone express concern or greater interest in them will cause the person to react negatively. This makes it much harder for the person to develop any type of meaningful relationships because they deny people the opportunity to provide any type of support. This does protect them from relationships failing and the confusion that comes with having a relationship. However, it also means they are denied having all of the benefits from healthy relationships.

Understanding Dependency: The Spectrum from Counter-Dependency to Codependency

Humans are social creatures, so we are meant to have interdependence on each other. Studies have repeatedly shown that people who live in a community have longer lifespans. When people have healthy relationships with the people around them, developing proper give and take relationships, it helps them to thrive. However, there are unhealthy types of dependency that tend to lower a person's life expectancy and ability to thrive.

Interdependency

If you are interdependent, it means you are able to establish and maintain healthy relationships. People who have secure attachments are able to adapt to this kind of relationship with others. They don't rely solely on others for their survival and health, but they understand the value of maintaining good relationships. If you are interdependent on others, you know how to offer support and ask for it before things get to a breaking point.

Codependent

People who have anxious attachments or disorganized attachments are much more likely to develop codependent relationships. That means that in a relationship, one person does most of the giving, and the other person gives very little into the relationship. A person may be on either end of the relationship, although people who are anxiously attached are much more likely to be the givers and disorganized attachment is much more likely to benefit without having to give as much.

Despite popular ideas about codependency, it is more than simply being overly reliant on one person. The people's lives are so enmeshed in each other that they have trouble operating if the other person isn't available to help them. They have trouble identifying themselves outside of the relationship. There is an unhealthy need to be with other people, and without the relationship, you are more likely to feel unlovable or empty. Their sense of self-worth is tied up in the relationship, even if they are capable of having a job and doing things independently. The giver in the relationship is constantly working to earn the love they feel they don't deserve. The taker in the relationship has a need to control and take. There is a twisted sense of love that is unhealthy to an outside observer, but to those in the relationship, it is how things need to be for them to be happy and fulfilled.

Counter-dependency

People with an avoidant attachment style tend to exhibit counter-dependency. They constantly push people away from them because they don't feel that they can rely on them. Where someone who is codependent often exhibits a lot of vulnerability and weakness, someone who is counter-dependent appears strong almost to the point of being invulnerable. They tend to appear self-confident and competent in most situations. They are more likely to blame others for problems if they had to rely on them, largely because they expect that problems arise when they are forced to interact with others.

People who are codependent are more likely to display signs of being a victim, but the counter-dependent person tends to victimize others in an effort to avoid being hurt first. They may have controlling tendencies because they don't trust others to do things right.

Strategies for Managing Dependency in Relationships

Like attachment styles, you have to learn to understand how you tend to behave in relationships. To better manage your relationships, The following will help you to better manage your relationships.

1. Pay attention to how you behave with others. Is there a person whom you feel you must have in your life, or do you feel that you can't let anyone get close to you? Typically, this isn't something you chose to feel, but something that you learn to feel over time.

2. Work toward building your self-esteem. Most people who are codependent don't feel they have an identity outside of their relationship, and this is often because they don't have much self-esteem. It's important to start acknowledging the positive things about yourself. Other people outside of the codependent relationship may be able to help you see those positives. You can also start to learn new skills that you can apply outside of the relationship or to set

goals that help to improve your life outside of who you are with the person or persons who are part of the codependent relationship.

For people who are counter-dependent, it is good to reflect on areas where you can start building your self-esteem when it comes to emotions. You have to learn to connect to them and to be more aware, to allow yourself to have them without feeling that it means you are wea.

3. Establish boundaries. People in codependent relationships tend to ignore their boundaries. For people who develop counter-dependent relationships, it's important to understand where your boundaries are so you can anticipate what could trigger strong emotional reactions that result in you either feeling panicked or anxious.

   In order to better understand your boundaries, you might start by asking yourself questions. For example, determine what actions make you feel unhappy or upset? What happened over the course of the last day that you ended up doing that you didn't want to, or that you wished you would have done differently?

4. Practice being assertive or engaging in more productive communication. This applies to both types of dependency because both types tend to ignore honest conversations. Take the time to learn to talk about your emotions openly. This won't be easy because there are problems for both types of dependency when it comes to talking about emotions. Codependent people tend to feel no one will listen or that their feelings aren't valid. Counter-dependent people aren't accustomed to acknowledging their emotions, let alone being able to talk about those emotions.

5. Take the time to be self-reflective and mindful of your situation. The following questions can help you to understand yourself and how you form relationships with others.

   a. When you are alone, how do you manage to care for yourself?
   b. Do you feel someone is draining you physically, emotionally, or financially?
   c. Do you find yourself regretting saying "yes" or "no" to things that you regret later? And does this happen often?
   d. Do you feel resentful toward people in your life because you feel you help them more than they help you? Or because they ask more of you than you feel comfortable to give?
   e. Do you often neglect yourself as your lowest priority? Or do you neglect your emotions entirely because they are too difficult to confront?

6. Take the time to calm yourself and address your emotions on your own. It's important to spend time processing your emotions. For people who are codependent, you need to do this without anyone else's input or interpretation. For people who are counter-dependent, you have to learn to acknowledge and understand your emotions.

Exercise: Reflect on Discomfort with Dependency in Relationships

Objective:

This exercise encourages you to explore and reflect on your feelings and experiences regarding dependency within relationships. By examining moments when dependency made you uncomfortable, you can gain insights into your boundaries, needs, and expectations in relationships.

Instructions:

Prompt 1: Identifying the Moment

Think back to a specific time when you felt uncomfortable due to the level of dependency in a relationship (this could be a romantic relationship, a friendship, or a family relationship). Describe the situation briefly.

Your Response:

_____

_____

_____

_____

_____

Prompt 2: Analyzing Your Feelings

Reflect on how you felt during this time. Were you feeling trapped, overwhelmed, or perhaps indifferent? Try to pinpoint the emotions and thoughts that were going through your mind.

Your Response:

_____

_____

_____

_____

_____

Prompt 3: Understanding Your Reaction

Consider how you reacted to the situation. Did you withdraw, communicate your feelings, or perhaps react in a way that surprised you? Describe your response and any actions you took.

Your Response:

_____

_____

_____

_____

_____

Prompt 4: Learning from the Experience

What did this experience teach you about your comfort levels with dependency in relationships? Identify any patterns or boundaries that this situation highlighted for you.

Your Response:

_____

_____

_____

_____

_____

Prompt 5: Future Steps

Based on this reflection, what steps would you like to take in future relationships to manage your comfort with dependency? Consider how you might communicate your needs or boundaries differently.

Your Response:

_____

_____

_____

_____

_____

Outcome:

This exercise aims to provide a platform for introspection on how dependency affects your relationships. By understanding your reactions and comfort levels, you can work towards healthier relationship dynamics that respect both your needs and the needs of others.

Exercise: Map Out Your Family's Attachment Styles

Objective:

This exercise is designed to help you explore and understand the attachment styles present within your family and how these styles have potentially influenced your own attachment behavior. Recognizing these patterns can offer insights into your interpersonal relationships and guide you toward more secure attachments.

Instructions:

Step 1: Identify Family Members

List the key family members you interact with regularly or who have had a significant impact on your life. This can include parents, siblings, grandparents, or any other influential figures from your upbringing.

Step 2: Observing Attachment Styles

For each family member listed, consider their behaviors and tendencies in relationships based on your observations and experiences. Try to identify which attachment style (secure, avoidant, anxious, or disorganized) best describes each person. Note that these are your perceptions and may not perfectly categorize each individual.

Family Member - Attachment Style - Observations:

- *Family Member 1:* _____
    - *Attachment Style:* _____
    - *Observations:* _____

- *Family Member 2:* _____
    - *Attachment Style:* _____
    - *Observations:* _____

Step 3: Reflect on Influences

Reflect on how the attachment styles of these family members have influenced your own way of forming and maintaining relationships. Consider both positive influences and challenges.

Prompt 1: Positive Influences

Describe any positive influences on your attachment style from family members. How have their behaviors or approaches to relationships benefited your own attachment behaviors?

Your Response:

_____

_____

_____

_____

Prompt 2: Challenges

Describe any challenges or difficulties in forming secure attachments that may have stemmed from your family's attachment styles. How have these influenced your expectations or behaviors in relationships?

Your Response:

_____

_____

_____

_____

Prompt 3: Patterns and Repetitions

Identify any patterns or repeated behaviors in your family's attachment styles that you see manifesting in your own relationships. How do you feel about these patterns?

Your Response:

_____

_____

_____

_____

Step 4: Considering Change

Based on this mapping and reflection, consider any changes you might want to make in your own attachment behaviors. Are there aspects of your family's styles that you wish to emulate or avoid? How can you work towards these changes?

Prompt 4: Desired Changes

Identify specific aspects of your attachment style you'd like to change or improve upon, inspired by this exercise. What steps can you take to foster these changes?

Your Response:

_____

_____

_____

_____

Outcome:

This exercise aims to deepen your understanding of the familial influences on your attachment style. By mapping out these patterns and reflecting on their impact, you can gain clarity on your relational behaviors and work towards fostering healthier attachments in your life.

Practical Exercise: Practice Expressing Needs in a Relationship Without Fear of Dependency

Objective:

The aim of this exercise is to enhance your comfort level in expressing your needs within a relationship, thereby reducing the fear of creating dependency. This practice is essential for fostering healthy, balanced relationships where communication and mutual support are valued.

Instructions:

1. **Identify Your Needs:** Take some time to reflect on your needs that you may have been hesitant to express in your relationships. These can range from emotional support, space, or specific actions from your partner or friend.
2. **Choose the Right Moment:** Find a calm and comfortable time when you and your partner or friend are likely to be receptive and open to discussion. Avoid times of stress or conflict.

3. **Express Your Needs Clearly:** Use "I" statements to express your needs clearly and assertively. For example, say "I feel valued when we spend quality time together," instead of "You don't spend enough time with me." This approach helps in taking ownership of your feelings and needs without placing blame.

4. **Discuss and Negotiate:** Be open to hearing the other person's thoughts and feelings. Remember, expressing your needs is the first step; the next is to discuss how these can be met within the dynamics of your relationship.

5. **Monitor Your Feelings:** Pay attention to how you feel before, during, and after expressing your needs. Note any feelings of discomfort, anxiety, or relief. Reflect on these feelings to understand your relationship with dependency and autonomy.

Outcome:

Through this exercise, you aim to become more adept at communicating your needs without the fear of being perceived as dependent. It encourages a healthy dynamic in relationships where both parties feel comfortable expressing their needs and working together to meet them.

Practical Exercise: Set Boundaries in a Current Relationship and Observe Your Emotional Responses

Objective:

This exercise focuses on setting clear boundaries in one of your current relationships and observing your emotional responses to these actions. The goal is to understand how establishing boundaries affects your sense of independence and emotional well-being in relationships.

Instructions:

1. **Identify the Boundary:** Reflect on a boundary that you feel is necessary to establish in a current relationship. This could relate to your time, emotional space, physical space, or any aspect that is important to your personal well-being.

2. **Plan Your Communication:** Think about how you will communicate this boundary. Be clear and concise in your explanation, and use "I" statements to express how this boundary is important for your well-being.

3. **Communicate the Boundary:** Choose an appropriate time to discuss this boundary with the person involved. Explain why this boundary is important to you and how you believe it will benefit your relationship.

4. **Observe and Reflect:** After setting the boundary, observe your own emotional responses. Do you feel relieved, anxious, guilty, or empowered? Write down your feelings and any reactions from the other person.

5. **Evaluate the Outcome:** Reflect on the effectiveness of the boundary. Consider whether it has been respected and how it has impacted your relationship. Think about any adjustments that may be necessary to ensure the boundary is maintained.

Outcome:

By setting boundaries and observing your emotional responses, you aim to foster a greater understanding of your needs and how asserting these needs affects your relationships. This exercise promotes self-awareness and the importance of boundaries in maintaining healthy, respectful, and fulfilling relationships.

Chapter 3

THE AVOIDANT EXPERIENCE IN RELATIONSHIPS

Being in a relationship as someone who is avoidant attachment is incredibly difficult because you never really feel safe in a relationship. Your inability to trust people to do things and your desire to protect yourself make it all but impossible to form an attachment. The emotional distance may feel initially comfortable, but it can also prevent you from feeling fulfilled. People who have avoidant experiences are more likely to paint past relationships in a better light or to realize too late that someone could have been a good match for them. The constant desire to find "the one" will inevitably end in them learning that "the one" doesn't exist. Unlike most people  though, it isn't because the concept is ridiculous, but because there is something "wrong" with the person who has this type of attachment style.

Emotional Distance: Navigating the Challenges

Being emotionally detached means that you are either unwilling or unable to connect with people emotionally, but you are also unable to understand or process your own emotions. Essentially, you've built a wall between yourself and others so that they cannot harm you. While this does present that one some level, it means that you fail to have the kinds of support that you can get with people who can understand you and help you work through your issues. The coping mechanism that helped you through childhood is undermining you in adulthood because you are unable to give people a chance to disappoint you the way your caregiver did.

People who are disorganized may also create emotional distance, although it is often because they have learned to shut down to avoid being further traumatized.

Establishing emotional distance does have its place. That is exactly the point of establishing boundaries or keeping a distance from people who tend to bring out the worst in you. Even people who have secure attachments can create emotional distance to protect themselves. The difference is that when they are more emotionally detached, it isn't because they don't care or are trying to protect themselves from *any* harm. It's because they understand themselves and their interactions with people. They have firm boundaries, and they ensure people remain on the right side of those boundaries. There will be people who are allowed within those boundaries because they are seen as safe and caring. For example, when they marry, they allow one person to fulfill a very close role and play a vital part in their life. There will still be boundaries, but the person with the secure attachment trusts the other person to respect those boundaries once they are expressed. The most common would be not to sleep over at the house of an ex. This is an understood rule, so a good partner will know not to do this without the boundary having to be stated. The boundaries are logical and based on trust.

This is very different compared to the avoidant attachment because the boundaries are so large as to always exclude everyone. The point of the boundaries isn't about establishing a comfort level that makes sense, but to prevent any kind of emotional attachment from forming. It's counter-productive to having a relationship since on one is allowed on the other side of some enormous boundaries.

This book is designed to help you learn how to establish boundaries that are healthier and to manage though. While you shouldn't simply trust people right off the bat, you don't need to adopt an approach that entirely prevents people from getting close to you. Trust should be something you learn to build with others, instead of refusing to trust anyone.

The Idealization of Partners and the Phantom Ex Syndrome

A large problem with people with this attachment style is that they tend to have an idea of what the perfect person is in their head. They believe they know exactly what they want and that is what they look for in a partner. They are much more likely to buy into the idea of there being "the one" who will make life good. And only a person who meets an incredibly high bar can be "the one."

Of course, this is a recipe for disaster because "the one" is a myth that simply doesn't exist. All relationships are work, and even the most idyllic relationships require the two people to work at it every day. Some relationships are easier than others, but there will always be difficulties that come up and people will have different opinions on things. As long as you agree on the most important stuff and avoid letting little, unimportant things get in the way, a relationship is possible with any number of people. There is no single person who can fill that role for you. It is about compatibility and the ability to compromise.

For someone who is avoidant attached, they spend most of the relationship looking for the one flaw that someone has that makes them not "the one," and once they see it, the relationship is over. This is why they often have a lot more relationships that do not last long. No one can possibly meet such a high bar expectation because what the person is looking for is perfection. It's an impossible ideal that does not work in reality.

Over time, you are more likely to start looking back at your relationships and come to a very negative conclusion. Many people either believe that "the one" doesn't exist so there is no reason to keep trying to find them. In these cases, the person may become very jaded and will either use people to meet basic needs or will withdraw entirely. Others may start to look back over their relationships and start to idealize a past partner. That one relationship can be built up so big in their mind that it becomes "clear" to the person that they missed their shot at a real romance.

When you find yourself fixated on a past ex, this is called the phantom ex. You start to remember things differently or to romanticize the way things were. This is actually a problem for all types of attachment styles, but given how quickly avoidantly attached people go through relationships, they do have pretty good odds of having a phantom ex. As a result, people who are avoidant tend to change a past relationship into something that it wasn't, usually because they didn't let the person get close enough. That person becomes "the one who got away," even though the majority of the time the relationship was almost certainly dysfunctional.

Relationship Dynamics with Insecure Attachments: Avoidant, Anxious, and Disorganized

People with secure attachments may have an easier time with relationships, but they need to be aware of the dynamics with people who have different attachment styles because they will very likely end up with someone who has an insecure attachment style. Perhaps the relationship will not be romantic, but they will have people in their family, friend group, or at work who will have a very different dynamic with others because of how they attach to others.

If a person has an anxious attachment style, they require a lot of validation and reassurance that you care. It can be exhausting because it can seem like nothing you say or do will ever be enough. They are insecure and often fear that you will abandon them, and they will feel that they deserve it. When you do something wrong, they will believe it is their fault. This can make it more challenging to talk to them as they may not listen when you try to help them see it's not necessarily anyone's fault. Or at least it probably isn't solely their fault. Their insecurities tend to be the reason for breakups, which is sad because it is more of a self-fulfilling prophecy. If they can learn to be more confident and feel more secure, most of the time people would stay with them.

People with a disorganized attachment style tend to be more chaotic in their emotions and expressions of their emotions. Their behavior may come across as bizarre or contradictory as they swing from one extreme to another. They may react from a place of trauma, then try to fix that by overcompensating. They need to start addressing the trauma that causes their more unpredictable behaviors so that they can start building better foundations for their relationships.

If you are avoidant attached, odds are very high that you have been called a commitment-phobe and been told that you are too cold. You tend to avoid dealing with conflict, which can be really upsetting to a partner who wants to resolve a problem. This means that problems and conflicts may stack up until the person with the insecure attachment simply pulls out of the relationship entirely. The primary issue is a lack of communication, so it is important to learn to start understanding your emotions and learn how to communicate them.

The Dynamics of Attraction and Distance in Relationships

The power dynamics of any relationship refers to the roles that the people play within that relationship. It doesn't have to refer to romantic relationships, as a parent and child can have a distancer/pursuer relationships where the parent is aloof and the child constantly strives to earn approval. Much of what is covered here can pertain to other types of relationships, but it is often considered in more romantic relationships.

There are three primary types of power dynamics in relationships:

- Demand and withdrawal
- Distance and pursuer
- Fear and shame

Your attachment style often plays into what kind of dynamic you have, and what role you assume in a relationship. Remember that it isn't about one person being dominant and the other submissive, but about how people act within the relationship.

Demand and Withdrawal

If you are in a demand and withdrawal dynamic, one of the partners often feels that their wants and needs are not addressed or taken into account by their partner. The person who makes the demands often feels that they can't get through to their partner, no matter how many times they ask. This often leads to resentment and frustration.

The other partner tends to withdraw and avoid conflict. This person tends to have an avoidant attachment style, but not always. It is possible that they are simply failing to communicate the boundaries they are trying to set, leaving their partner feeling ignored. Sometimes, it is an act of rebellion because they feel that their partner is making too many demands.

Often there are numerous, unimportant fights in the relationship. It's incredibly unhealthy and neither party is happy. The best solution is to develop better communication on both ends. It also requires commitment from both parties to working to be more effective in their communication, such as saying, "I feel that I require more support for a particular situation. What are you willing to do to assist me?" Or for the person who is withdrawing, they can say something along the lines of, "I feel that you are disappointed in me. Can we sit down and discuss the expectations?" When you sit down to talk about the situation, you must remain calm and talk in a respectful way. This can be very difficult if you've built up a negative way of speaking to each other.

Distance and Pursuer

Usually this type of dynamic is reflective of one person being far more committed and the other feeling less invested in the relationship. The pursuer partner may want to constantly communicate with the other, so will text several times over the course of the day. The distance partner may feel stifled by this constant contact.

The pursuer may be someone with an anxious attachment style, but they don't have to be. Some people have a much more overt love language, so that connection is something they enjoy. The distance may be someone with an avoidant or disorganized style, but not always. It is possible that someone with a secure attachment has a different way of expressing love and interest, such as doing it in person instead of over devices.

Communication is important, but both sides need to learn to get out of their comfort zone if they want the relationship to work. The pursuer may need to pull back and allow the distance partner to do more initiating, including setting up plans for dates or activities. The distance person needs to be more obviously engaged so that the pursuer doesn't feel all the work is on them. It's about thinking of the other person and what will make *them* happy, even if it isn't exactly your love language.

Fear and Shame

At least one partner is likely to be insecure and very likely have considerable emotional pain from previous relationships. Often one partner has more anxiety and fear about how secure they are in the relationship. The other may feel ashamed of the level of contact and attention, resulting in them avoiding their partner.

At the root is usually trauma at least for one partner, if not both.

To overcome this type of dynamic requires a lot of trust building and allowing each other to be vulnerable. This may require some space or distance to process what has been said or expressed. Work to make your partner feel that you are a safe space so they feel supported. This works for both sides. For example, the shame may come from the partner's body image, leading to them pulling away from their partner. This triggers fear in their partner. This creates a vicious cycle that requires better communication and support between the partners.

Avoidance Attachment in Love and Relationships

It's important to keep all of this in mind when you go into a romantic relationship. All of what we've covered so far is true of someone who is avoidant attached when in a romantic relationship, but it is much harder not to take it personally. The problem is that it is difficult to feel that there is a reason to get really emotionally invested in a romantic relationship. Getting attached to any real level is seen as a way of ensuring that they are hurt, which is even worse than just being disappointed.

As a result, people who have an avoidant attachment style tend to keep relationships from becoming deeper than a very surface level. Since they often come across as gregarious and easy to get along with, people tend to want to date people with this attachment style. This means that the person isn't concerned about getting into a relationship - there will almost always be someone ready to try to engage with them romantically. The problem comes when someone tries to get a commitment out of the person. Once they are pressed to start being more committed or pressed to be more open and vulnerable, the person with the avoidant attachment style will start to pull back, and often they will end up breaking up with their partner because they don't feel like it will be worth their time and energy. While they justify it as it being best to break it off now to avoid leading someone on, most of the time the reality is that they are more concerned about being vulnerable with someone.

The level of intimacy that they are willing to engage in can vary a lot. Some avoid physical intimacy, while others are comfortable having a lot of largely meaningless sexual relationships. Some find it difficult to allow themselves to be as vulnerable as they would need to be to become physically intimate. Others don't view that kind of vulnerability as being particularly risky, which allows them to feel like they are getting close. They are offering more to their partners, even if it is not something they do in a way to foster a deeper relationship.

People with this attachment style tend to have several reasons that they tell themselves to refrain from getting too close to people:

- They don't know someone well enough to open up to them. This is ironic because by never opening up, they ensure that they never know people well enough to open up. It's a self-fulfilling prophecy that keeps them from getting close to anyone.
- They often buy into the idea that there is one person for everyone, and that is something they hold onto well into adulthood. What has them let go of this concept is the fact that they never meet the one, in which case they will decide there is no one out there for them. They fail to grasp that all healthy relationships require both parties to be open and committed. This means being able to trust the other person enough to open up to them. Healthy relationships start by building trust and learning how trustworthy a person is. Someone who is avoidantly attached to their romantic partner doesn't allow this process to start, at least not from their side.
- They spend most of their time looking for faults. Since they are hung up on finding "one" person to be their forever partner, they will bail on a relationship at the first fight or when they see something in their partner that they do not like. As often as not, they will look for

a flaw to justify ending the relationship as soon as the partner starts asking for a deeper relationship.

- The more a person tries to talk to them about problems, or worse emotions, the more they will draw away, accusing the person of pushing too much or overstepping boundaries. While boundaries are necessary in every relationship, the way that avoidantly attached people establish them ensures that no one gets close to them. Boundaries are used as a way to keep people away, which is not what boundaries should do.

Chapter 9 goes into a lot more detail about how people in romantic relationships act both as someone who is avoidantly attached and as a partner with someone who has that attachment style. The section The Pursuit of Perfection and the Reality of Imperfection in Partnerships provides details about how to navigate this kind of relationship, and if you want to be involved with someone with this attachment style, it will provide you with the information you need to respect the boundaries. You should be working in tandem with the person who is avoidantly attached so that you can both be aware of what the other is doing. It should help you to better work to maintain boundaries that allow the person to feel safe as they learn to feel safer with you.

For now, it is important to understand how someone who is avoidantly attached to others views them in a romantic relationship. Often they actually do want to have someone in their lives, but they hold themselves back. They may not realize that they actually want someone, even though they know they are looking for "the one." Instead of getting particularly upset, they are more likely to say that it's fine, they don't actually need anyone else, then instead of trying to form a meaningful partnership, they will decide that short-term relationships are more than enough for them.

Their apparent indifference to emotions isn't personal, and it doesn't mean that they don't have emotions, especially when it comes to a romantic relationship. The problem is that they aren't really equipped to deal with emotions, so they are likely to have a negative reaction to those emotions. Since they don't really know how to help people cope with their emotions, and they don't want their significant other to hurt, they retreat, feeling someone else will be better able to deal with the emotions of their loved ones. As someone they care about starts to feel heightened emotions, it is more likely to make the person with this attachment style will start to feel stressed. In some cases, they have to leave before their stress levels get too high and they have a panic attack. While there is some element of protecting themselves from getting close to others, it's also possible that they are protecting themselves from the kind of stress emotions cause them.

Being in a romantic relationship is going to be very difficult because of these relationships' nature means going outside of their comfort zone and getting emotionally attached to someone. It requires a lot more trust and emotional regulation than they are likely to be able to manage. This does not mean it isn't possible. Simply knowing that this is your attachment style can go a long way to starting to change how you interact and attach to others. Even though you probably tel yourself you are fine on your own, the vast majority of people with this attachment style actually do want a meaningful relationship. They settle for less because they feel that there is something wrong with them or everyone else that will make it impossible. The constant saying that they are fine alone gives them a permission base to keep being alone, even if that isn't what they actually want. It's one way to justify something that they feel is inevitable anyway, which actually prevents them from having the kind of deep romantic relationships that they want if they find "the one," and at the same time feeling that it will never happen.

Exercise: Journal About a Time You Felt Emotional Walls Come Up and What Triggered Them

Objective:

This exercise invites you to reflect on moments when you've instinctively put up emotional barriers. By exploring these instances and their triggers, you can gain insights into your protective mechanisms, understand your avoidant tendencies better, and consider steps towards more open and fulfilling relationships.

Instructions:

Prompt 1: Identifying the Moment

Think of a specific time when you felt your emotional walls go up in a relationship or interaction. This could be a moment of potential vulnerability, conflict, or when intimacy (emotional or physical) was expected.

Your Response:

_____

_____

_____

_____

_____

Prompt 2: Exploring the Trigger

Reflect on what triggered these emotional walls. Was it something said or done by the other person, a feeling of vulnerability, a memory of a past experience, or perhaps the fear of getting too close? Describe the trigger as best as you can.

Your Response:

_____

_____

_____

_____

_____

Prompt 3: Understanding Your Reaction

Analyze how you reacted both internally and externally. Did you withdraw, change the subject, express anger, or shut down communication? How did this reaction serve to protect you, and what was it protecting you from?

Your Response:

_____

_____

_____

_____

_____

Prompt 4: Reflecting on the Aftermath

Consider the aftermath of this incident. How did your reaction affect the relationship or interaction? Did it create distance, misunderstandings, or perhaps even a resolution of some kind?

Your Response:

_____

_____

_____

_____

_____

Prompt 5: Contemplating Change

Now that you've reflected on this moment and your protective mechanisms, think about how you might want to handle similar situations in the future. Are there healthier ways you can envision responding to such triggers?

Your Response:

_____

_____

_____

Outcome:

This exercise aims to encourage self-reflection on the moments when you've erected emotional barriers, why they occurred, and how they've impacted your relationships. By understanding these patterns, you can work towards more consciously managing your reactions and fostering deeper, more authentic connections with others.

Exercise: Reflect on Idealizing Partners and Its Impact on Your Relationships

Objective:

This exercise aims to guide you in reflecting on how the pattern of idealizing partners has shaped your expectations and experiences in relationships. Understanding this tendency can help you navigate future relationships with more realistic expectations, contributing to healthier and more fulfilling connections.

Instructions:

Step 1: Recognizing Idealization

Think about a time or multiple times when you caught yourself idealizing a partner or potential partner. Describe the qualities or aspects of the person that you idealized.

Your Response:

_____

_____

_____

Step 2: Comparison with Reality

Reflect on how the idealized image of the partner compared with their real behavior and personality over time. Were there discrepancies? How did you feel when faced with these discrepancies?

Your Response:

_____

_____

_____

_____

Step 3: Impact on the Relationship

Consider how idealizing this person impacted your relationship. Did it lead to disappointment, frustration, or perhaps a lack of seeing the person for who they truly are? Describe the effect on both your feelings and the dynamics of the relationship.

Your Response:

_____

_____

_____

_____

Step 4: Self-Reflection on Needs and Fears

Reflect on what your tendency to idealize may reveal about your own needs, fears, or insecurities. For example, does it reflect a fear of being alone, a desire for a perfect companion to avoid dealing with personal issues, or perhaps an avoidance of genuine intimacy?

Your Response:

_____

_____

_____

_____

Step 5: Moving Forward

Based on your reflections, think about steps you can take to approach future relationships with a more grounded and realistic perspective. How can you balance hope and excitement with a clear-sighted view of the other person's humanity and imperfections?

Your Response:

_____

_____

_____

_____

Outcome:

Through this exercise, you aim to gain a deeper understanding of how idealizing partners affects your approach to relationships and yourself. Recognizing and addressing this pattern can lead to more genuine connections, where you appreciate and love someone for who they are, not just for who you want them to be.

Practical Exercise: Initiate a Conversation About Emotional Needs with a Partner or Close Friend

Objective:

The goal of this exercise is to enhance open communication about emotional needs with someone close to you. This practice is crucial for deepening understanding, empathy, and connection in your relationships, particularly if you tend to maintain emotional distance.

Instructions:

1. **Preparation:** Think about what your emotional needs are at this moment in your life. Are you seeking more support, understanding, time together, or perhaps space?
2. **Choose the Right Moment:** Select a comfortable and private time for both of you, ensuring you won't be interrupted or distracted. It's important that both of you are in a receptive state of mind.
3. **Express Your Needs:** Begin the conversation with appreciation for the relationship. Use "I" statements to express your needs clearly, such as "I feel valued and loved when we spend quality time together."

4. **Listen Actively:** Encourage them to share their emotional needs as well. Listen actively, without judgment, ensuring they feel heard and understood.

5. **Mutual Understanding:** Discuss how both sets of needs can be met. This might involve compromise or finding new ways to support each other.

6. **Follow-Up:** Make this type of conversation a regular part of your relationship to continuously nurture and strengthen your bond.

Outcome:

This exercise aims to foster a stronger emotional connection by openly discussing needs, which is often a challenging area for those with avoidant attachment styles. By regularly engaging in these conversations, you can build a more secure and mutually supportive relationship.

Practical Exercise: Commit to a Small Act That Decreases Emotional Distance in a Relationship

Objective:

This exercise is designed to take a proactive step towards closing the emotional distance often present in relationships where one or both parties have avoidant tendencies. The act should be something that conveys warmth, care, and connection.

Instructions:

1. **Identify the Act:** Think of a small, meaningful act that can help bridge the emotional gap between you and a loved one. This could be anything from writing a heartfelt note, setting aside quality time to spend together, or showing interest in something important to them.

2. **Plan Your Act:** Consider how and when you will carry out this act. Planning ensures that your effort is thoughtful and tailored to the person's preferences and needs.

3. **Execution:** Carry out your act of kindness or connection. Remember, the goal is to express care and reduce emotional distance, so focus on the gesture's emotional significance rather than its grandeur.

4. **Observe the Reaction:** Observe the reaction of others to the deed. Note any changes in the emotional atmosphere of your relationship.

5. **Reflect:** After completing the act, take some time to reflect on how it made you feel. Did it change your perspective on emotional closeness? How did it affect your relationship?

6. **Consistency:** Consider making these acts a regular part of your interaction with loved ones to continuously work on closing the emotional distance.

Outcome:

This exercise aims to show the power of small, considerate acts in nurturing relationships and decreasing emotional distance. By consciously choosing to connect in meaningful ways, you can take steps towards more emotionally fulfilling relationships.

Chapter 4

COMMUNICATION AND EMOTIONAL BARRIERS

Communication is often the biggest hurdle that someone with an avoidant attachment style will face. They have little experience communicating important information, particularly for personal issues. They may be fantastic communicators at work when roles are clearly defined and expectations are set, but these are skills that do not translate to their personal lives since roles are never so clean cut.

The biggest problem with communication is getting through their emotional barriers, which not only block out everyone in their lives, emotions are usually blocked to the person themselves.

Working to develop more secure attachments means focusing on these two areas and working to be more emotionally vulnerable and communicative with the people around you.

Communication Barriers: Avoiding Deep Conversations and Requests for Reassurance

Since they are so detached from their own emotions, there is very little chance that someone with this attachment style will be able to communicate with others. It is much easier to avoid any deep, meaningful conversations because that will lead to rising emotions. And that is simply too much unnecessary work. It is easier to hold shallow, friendly conversations where there is no risk of really getting to know someone. As a result, they can't possibly let you down as you never had much expectation for them.

Another reason to avoid deep conversations is because it means people won't be able to criticize you on a more meaningful level. If someone doesn't know you well enough to form a real opinion of you, then whatever criticism they have isn't going to be valid. This provides a layer of protection for you.

Part of this also means that you never feel that you can ask for reassurance. If people don't really know you or have appropriate criticisms, they can't possibly provide you reassurance for the same reason. It adds yet another layer of communication barrier.

The real problem is that these barriers ensure that you can never draw close to people. You don't trust them to form proper opinions, so their takes don't matter. It means that they can never get to know you well enough to help you, even when you need it.

One problem always drives the other, constantly exacerbating the problem. To break down the barriers requires learning to both have deep conversations and to learn to ask for help. Neither will be easy, so it will take time. Ultimately, it is worth it though.

Tools for Overcoming Avoidance and Building Closer Ties

Sometimes it can help to focus on tools to start working to break down emotional and communication barriers. The following are a few that you can start to use to see what will work for you.

1. Become more aware of what triggers you to try to avoid a situation or person. You aren't going to be expected to immediately change, and you definitely should not force yourself to stay in a situation where you aren't comfortable. However, you should be learning what triggers this reaction. Avoidance is something you use as a tool to alleviate stress and emotions. You need to understand what caused the stress and emotion so you can start to manage it more effectively.

2. Once you have an idea of what triggers your avoidant reaction, start to simulate the experience in your mind to try to create a different end result. You don't have to imagine

something extremely different. It can be small things you can do to start working toward the larger changes. It's similar to working toward running in a marathon. If you don't currently run, you start with walking more often, then you do a 5k, and continue to work up to the marathon. When dealing with an insecure attachment, you have to learn to think through situations to retrain your brain from going to your current solution – avoidance of the situation. By breaking down the situation into small steps, you will be able to start taking those small steps in life to change your reaction. It's much easier with small actionable steps, and it is less likely to make you feel anxious than if you try to do everything all at once.

3. Start thinking of tasks you can do now to start changing your avoidant reaction. You've started to determine what you can do, now think about how to break them down into manageable tasks you are comfortable doing. You can even continue to break down tasks if you find that you have taken on too much at one time.

4. Start to face your emotions and try to understand them. You are going to need to use affirmations to help yourself through this. As a child, you didn't get the kind of compassionate and empathetic support you needed to deal with your emotions, so you need to learn to give that to yourself now that you are an adult. Essentially, you are working to sooth your inner child who feels that emotions should be hidden and ignored. You are giving that child the permission to experience and deal with those emotions.

5. Practice mindfulness and meditation to learn to better control your physical reactions to emotions and triggering situations. By calming yourself, you can better control your nervous system. At this point, when you face something triggering, you essentially have a fight or flight response, and that means that your nervous system is driving your reaction. And your reaction is flight. Deep breaths and working to relax in these situations can help you better face them.

These tools can help you start to deal with your triggers and to face them without what has become your go-to reaction when facing conflict or emotions.

Building Trust and Emotional Connection

Trust is one of your biggest problems because you don't think that you can trust anyone but yourself. Without trust, no relationship will work for long. Up to this point, you've been refusing to build it, whether knowingly or unknowingly. As you build trust, you will start to build a better emotional connection as you learn that someone can be trusted.

1. Start with small promises and tasks. When you and your partner are able to fulfill them, you can see that the person actually can follow through. Over time, you can start to take on bigger tasks.

2. Try to communicate how you feel. You don't have to start with big things. Instead, you can talk about small stakes things, which you probably already do. This time start to talk about small things that have some emotion to them. For example, you can say that you are happy that your partner did something, which is a great way to show that you are noticing their actions. Instead of letting your negative emotions pileup, you can bring up something your partner did that you would like to discuss. Perhaps they texted you too often, made a comment that hurt you, or something minor they did. Don't start with big things, but little things that you can discuss with a little more confidence and comfort.

3. Don't make significant demands early – trust needs to be built up. You can't expect someone you've been dating for two months to commit to something four months away. You also shouldn't expect them to help you move or do something big. You can practice asking for help by letting them know, but don't expect them to just jump in.

4. Before making a decision, give it careful thought. Learn to stay on instead of entirely avoiding something.

5. Be consistent in your interactions and work on making communication about your emotions a part of that consistency.

6. Be honest with how you are feeling and why. Perhaps you don't know the why of your emotions yet, in which case you should ask for more time.

7. Openly admit when you make a mistake, and respect when your partner is able to admit their mistakes. Learning how to handle mistakes is an important part of building trust. It also shows your partner that you are willing to work with them after a mistake instead of just bailing.

Most of these are probably going to be a bit trying since you don't have a lot of experience allowing people close to you. The important thing is that you are working to establish trust, and it's the small steps that lead to more significant changes.

Assertiveness and Boundaries

Unlike other insecure attachments, you at least know where your boundaries are, even if those boundaries are incredibly wide. What's important is to start bringing those boundaries in so that people can get close to you. Instead of running from conflict, you need to learn to be more honest with how you are feeling. This means being assertive when you start to feel uncomfortable, instead of avoiding the topic entirely. You need to be honest with what your limitations and boundaries are so that people in your life are aware of why you are feeling triggered to take certain actions.

As someone who tends to avoid situations, you need to let people know that you need them to be patient. There is actually a lot of advice out there for telling people how to interact with someone who has an avoidant attachment style – more than there is for people with this style. That's because the style is repeatedly reinforced over time. If people understand your reactions, they can take proper actions to help you. This should only be done with people who are friends and family as they are the people who are best equipped to understand when you are starting to feel stressed. Hopefully they will also have the desire to help you heal.

That does not mean that you don't have just as much work. You just need people to be more active in the healing process since the beginning of the process is going to be incredibly difficult. You are working to overcome years or decades of a particular way of reacting. Having people who are willing to work with you and give you a safe space will allow you to start building trust.

Exercise: Draft a Difficult Conversation You've Been Avoiding and Outline Positive Outcomes

Objective:

This exercise is designed to help you confront and prepare for a difficult conversation that you've been avoiding, due to fear, anxiety, or uncertainty. By drafting this conversation and envisioning positive outcomes, you can reduce the emotional barriers that hinder communication in your relationships.

Instructions:

Step 1: Identify the Conversation

Think about a conversation you've been avoiding with someone important in your life. This could be addressing a conflict, expressing a need, or sharing feelings you've been holding back.

Your Conversation Topic:

_____

_____

_____

_____

_____

Step 2: Draft the Conversation

Write a script or bullet points for how you ideally want the conversation to go. Start with how you'll introduce the topic, express your feelings and needs clearly, and how you'll invite the other person to share their perspective. To concentrate on your emotions rather than placing blame or making accusations, use "I" phrases.

Your Conversation Draft:

_____

_____

_____

_____

_____

Step 3: Outline Positive Outcomes

Reflect on the best possible outcomes from having this conversation. How could it improve understanding, closeness, or resolve issues in your relationship? Describe specific positive changes you hope to see.

Positive Outcomes:

_____

_____

_____

_____

_____

Outcome:

This exercise aims to encourage proactive steps toward addressing and resolving issues that create emotional distance in your relationships. By preparing for the conversation and focusing on potential positive outcomes, you can approach it with more confidence and a clearer goal in mind, ultimately fostering healthier and more open communication.

Exercise: Identify Your Boundaries and Their Importance

Objective:

This exercise encourages you to explore and articulate your personal boundaries within relationships. Understanding and asserting your boundaries is crucial for maintaining your well-being and ensuring healthy interactions with others. By identifying why these boundaries are important to you, you can communicate them more effectively to those around you.

Instructions:

Step 1: Listing Your Boundaries

Begin by reflecting on what boundaries are essential for your emotional and physical well-being in relationships. These can range from needing personal space to how and when you prefer to communicate. List at least three boundaries that you feel are critical.

o   *Boundary:* _____

    ▪   *Why It's Important to Me:*

_____

_____

o   *Boundary:* _____

    ▪   *Why It's Important to Me:*

_____

_____

Step 2: Exploring the Origins

For each boundary listed, think about why it holds significance for you. Consider past experiences, your values, or aspects of your well-being that these boundaries protect.

Your Reflections:

o   *Boundary 1 Origin:* _____
o   *Boundary 2 Origin:* _____

_____

_____

_____

Step 3: Envisioning Respect for Boundaries

Imagine scenarios where your boundaries are respected. How does it make you feel? Why is it beneficial for your relationships when these boundaries are acknowledged and upheld?

Positive Scenarios and Feelings:

o   *Boundary 1:* _____
o   *Boundary 2:* _____

_____

_____

_____

Outcome:

Through this exercise, you aim to gain a deeper understanding of your personal boundaries and their significance to your emotional health and relationships. Recognizing and respecting your own boundaries is a step toward ensuring that they are respected by others, thereby fostering healthier and more fulfilling connections.

Practical Exercise: Practice Active Listening in Your Next Conversation

Objective:

By engaging in active listening, you will be able to improve your communication abilities. This is giving what is being said your all attention as opposed to just listening to what is being said. Prior to drafting a response, the goal is to comprehend the speaker's message.

Instructions:

1. **Choose a Conversation:** Decide on a forthcoming discussion in which you can deliberately engage in active listening. With a friend, relative, or coworker, for example.
2. **Prepare Mentally:** Approach the conversation with the intention to listen deeply. Remind yourself that your goal is to understand the speaker's perspective fully.
3. **Focus on the Speaker:** Give the speaker your full attention. Avoid distractions like looking at your phone or thinking about how you'll respond.
4. **Show You're Listening:** To demonstrate engagement, use nonverbal clues like nodding, keeping eye contact, and bending slightly forward.
5. **Hold Your Response:** Resist the urge to interrupt or formulate your response while the other person is speaking. Wait until they have finished their thought before you begin to speak.
6. **Clarify and Reflect:** After the speaker has finished, summarize what you've heard and ask clarifying questions if needed. This shows that you are trying to understand their perspective fully.
7. **Reflect on the Experience:** After the discussion, give yourself some time to consider how using active listening techniques improved the exchange. Did it change the depth of the conversation or your relationship with the speaker?

Outcome:

This exercise aims to improve your communication skills by focusing on active listening, fostering deeper understanding and connections in your relationships.

Practical Exercise: Express a Need or Boundary Clearly in a Relationship and Observe the Outcome

Objective:

This exercise encourages you to articulate a need or boundary within a relationship clearly. The aim is to observe the outcome and understand the importance of clear communication in maintaining healthy relationships.

Instructions:

1. **Identify a Need or Boundary:** Reflect on a current relationship where you need to express a specific need or boundary. Choose something meaningful to your well-being or the health of the relationship.
2. **Prepare Your Expression:** Think about how you can express this need or boundary clearly and respectfully. Use "I" statements to focus on your feelings and needs without placing blame.
3. **Choose the Right Moment:** Find an appropriate time to have this conversation, when both you and the other person are not preoccupied or stressed.
4. **Express Yourself:** Communicate your need or boundary to the other person. Be concise, clear, and assertive but also open to hearing their perspective.
5. **Observe the Outcome:** Pay attention to how the other person responds and how the conversation impacts your relationship. Note any changes in dynamics, understanding, or emotional closeness.
6. **Reflect:** Afterward, reflect on the experience. Consider what you learned about the importance of expressing your needs and boundaries and how doing so affects your relationships.

Outcome:

By clearly expressing your needs and boundaries, this exercise aims to enhance your ability to communicate effectively, leading to more respectful and mutually supportive relationships.

Chapter 5

THE PATH TO EMOTIONAL CONNECTION

As you start connecting with your emotions and learn how to communicate them to others, even on a really small scale, you start down the path to building emotional connections. This is why it's imperative that you actually learn to acknowledge your emotions and learn to deal with them. Until you process your emotions, it's very difficult to develop any kind of emotional connection to anyone else.

Understanding Fear of Intimacy

The fear of intimacy is a long-seated problem that is a result of lessons you learned as a child. Even as you seek to be closer to others, you push them away because you've learned that the connection won't last. On the one hand you are not alone, with between 15% and 20% of people showing signs of having a fear of intimacy. When people show that they are interested in getting to know you better, it is confusing because it can feel like they are demanding too much or that they have ulterior motives for wanting to get close to you.

The problem with this fear is that it keeps you isolated because you don't feel that people are sincere in their reasons for approaching you. This is perhaps ironic as it doesn't align with your greater independence and self-confidence, or apparent self-confidence. This is why people may see you as egotistical and self-centered. Your insecurities are pretty much just known to you, and you appear to lack any interest in letting anyone get close to you.

When you perceive something as a negative social cue, you are ready to drop the relationship entirely because it is more comfortable than becoming closer to someone. It is easier to be alone than to have to deal with negative emotions, and in some cases positive ones.

The problem is less about fearing intimacy, and more about being rejected. To avoid being rejected, you reject the other person.

Exploring Vulnerability

Learning to be vulnerable is going to feel unnatural and highly uncomfortable. You learned when you were little that emotions were meant to be repressed and ignored, so now you have a lot of discomfort when it comes to actually trying to connect with them. Even worse, they make you feel vulnerable. You are used to being a calm, collected person who is able to manage any situation. As you start to show that you *do* have emotions, it means that it will change how people see you. They will even have a better understanding of you, which you know means that they can start to use it against you if they don't mean you well. It means other people have more opportunities to hurt you because your weaknesses are now exposed.

Embracing vulnerability isn't easy for anyone with insecure attachments. It can even be difficult for people with secure attachments. The difference is that people with secure attachments know how to ask for help in a way that means people know how to support them.

You can get to that point, but it means allowing yourself to feel vulnerable with people. Don't set yourself up for failure by working with people you don't know well or who don't have your best interest at heart. This is one reason why finding a great therapist is a great idea for people with avoidant attachment. However, you can work on it on your own, at least initially.

When you start embracing your vulnerability, you need to know that it is a long process. The first steps are ones you can take on your own. This is the point where you start spending time reflecting on your own emotions, the ones that you have been ignoring. You will be uncomfortable with those emotions, and you will almost certainly feel that having them makes you weak. It doesn't. Instead of getting upset with yourself, do what people didn't do when you were young – practice compassion toward yourself. Your emotions are valid and there is a reason why you feel them. Emotions are meant to help you process the world, and they provide important information about the world around you. Learning to acknowledge your emotions will give you a lot of information about yourself. Just the act itself of facing your emotions will create an emotional reaction, which you can explore too.

Part of learning to be vulnerable is challenging your limiting beliefs. Something you've probably been telling yourself over the years is that you are better on your own, that you don't need anyone else, or that people can't be trusted. These statements are limiting yourself, as well as being largely untrue. There are very few absolute statements that are true, and people can't be trusted. It is a very serious absolute statement that has no merit. Yes, some people aren't trustworthy, but there are people out there who are. You have to learn to start building trust in others to determine if they can be trusted.

Strategies for Intimacy Enhancement

The most important thing to do is to realize what your triggers are. Up to this point when you are triggered, you often flee from the situation. By knowing that something is triggering the fight or flight response, you will be more aware that this is what is happening.

As difficult as it may be, to enhance intimacy you need to start sharing these triggers with people whom you consider important to you. If you have a romantic partner, that person knows that you have been triggered *before* you leave the situation. Good partners will understand that means you need space to deal with the spike in emotions or to settle your anxiety. Over time, they can help you to avoid feeling triggered by working to alleviate the distress before it reaches a point where you leave.

When you start to feel triggered, don't just leave. Let the person know that you need some personal space. All healthy relationships should allow for everyone to have time to themselves and to have space to deal with their feelings.

You also need to be selective in who you talk to about your emotions. As mentioned, not everyone can be trusted, so you do need to be selective about who you let into your healing process. One way to start determining a person's trustworthiness is to talk about inconsequential things. Pay attention to how the person reacts and if they talk to others about it. If that person is respectful of what you express and does not go telling people about what you said, you can start to talk about more important information, although you don't have to get into anything really significant yet. You are learning how to trust and to learn who is safe so that you can continue to build meaningful relationships. It is not going to be quick and easy – if it were, you wouldn't have developed the habits toward relationships that you currently have.

Think of developing intimacy with others as being a commitment to yourself first. You are committing to making your life better by learning how to develop more secure attachments. Since it is easier to rely on yourself, committing to working to make your life better can be a good way of looking at this process. You may have some negative emotions toward yourself, but you also know that you can rely on yourself. So trust yourself to start learning who can be trusted and start to build that trust when someone shows that they are capable of helping protect you and your emotions.

Finally, you have to learn to communicate. Sometimes the problem isn't' that someone isn't trustworthy, but that you two didn't properly communicate. You need to find a way to communicate that makes you feel safe. A person who is a good partner or can provide support will be able to help facilitate that safe space for you.

Building Mutual Respect and Trust

Building trust is never easy because the more life experience you have, the more stories you have of people being untrustworthy. Even people with secure attachments have to take a careful approach because trust is something that people must earn. It isn't something you should ever just give because the wrong kind of people will use it to their advantage.

However, there are good people out there who very likely can be trusted, and you are missing out by treating everyone the same without giving them a chance to earn your trust. This is just as true when it comes to respect. You should never respect people just because of who they are – they have to earn your respect.

Fortunately, building respect and trust can be done simultaneously, and the steps to do it are universal, no matter your attachment style. .The primary difference is that as someone with an avoidant attachment style, you may feel more uncomfortable because you are dealing with emotions and being put in situations that you often avoid. You should start small, but you can still use these steps to start slowly building the kinds of deeper relationships that will greatly benefit you over the course of your life.

1. Learn how to be an active listener. This means that you focus on what they are saying, not in determining what you should say next or how you should respond. Give the speaker your undivided attention, and if you need to talk, make it so that you are asking questions that gain clarification or details to better understand them. Do not interrupt them while they are speaking. This part may actually be easier for you as it does not require you to do much apart from listen. However, you must *listen* to them, and not allow your mind to wonder because what they are saying makes you uncomfortable because they are talking about their feelings. Being an active listener is what makes people trust you more, and it's why people tend to like avoidant attachments initially – they appear to be good listeners.

2. Start showing empathy for what people are saying. This is going to be far more difficult for you because you are less emotionally intelligent. Your disconnection to your feelings means that you may not always understand people's actions because of their emotions. Instead of judging them though, work to show that you understand on some levels, such as trying to see things from their perspective. This may be something that you learn to do much later in the process as you first need to come to terms with your own emotions before you can be empathetic toward others. At least that is often the case. When it comes to grieving over a loss, if you have lost someone, it will probably be easier to be empathetic because you have a one-to-one comparison to understand where they are coming from.

3. Start developing clear and respectful communication skills. Being a good listener is a part of this, but you also need to learn how to respond in ways that are clear too. Again, you need to understand your own emotional process before you can clearly communicate them, but not all communication is about emotions. You can work on being clearer in your communication at work where emotions are less likely to be relevant. Also, work to remove snide remarks, sarcasm, and other types of speech that are considered disrespectful. This makes people defensive and is much more likely to result in them being hostile instead of helpful.

4. Ask for and offer feedback. Criticism probably isn't something you take well, and you may not be particularly good at giving it. However, when people know that you are able to offer sound, constructive criticism, they will start to trust your judgment and outlook as they know that you are trying to help. Similarly, you will learn how to be less defensive as you see that people are offering you the same. And feedback doesn't have to be criticism. You can get positive feedback too. In fact, all feedback should have positive elements, even if there is criticism mixed into it. Feedback should foster a supportive environment where you feel that you can be honest and where you feel people are being honest in return.

Exercise: Write About a Fear of Intimacy You Have and Where You Think It Comes From

Objective:

This exercise encourages you to explore and articulate a specific fear of intimacy you experience, delving into its origins and understanding how it impacts your relationships. By identifying the root causes of this fear, you can begin to address and work through it.

Instructions:

Step 1: Identify the Fear

Reflect on your relationships and identify a specific fear of intimacy you have noticed. This could be a fear of being vulnerable, fear of rejection, or fear of losing your independence, among others.

Fear of Intimacy:

_____

_____

_____

_____

_____

Step 2: Trace Its Origins

Think about where this fear might have originated. Consider your past relationships, childhood experiences, or any pivotal moments that could have contributed to this fear.

Origin of Fear:

_____

_____

_____

_____

_____

Step 3: Impact on Relationships

Reflect on how this fear of intimacy has influenced your behavior in relationships. Consider specific instances where it prevented you from forming deeper connections.

Impact on Relationships:

_____

_____

_____

_____

_____

Outcome:

By completing this exercise, you aim to gain insights into your fear of intimacy, its roots, and its effects on your relationships. This understanding is a crucial step towards overcoming the fear and fostering deeper, more meaningful connections.

Exercise: List Ways You Can Show Vulnerability in a Relationship and the Fears Associated with Each

Objective:

This exercise is designed to help you consider different ways to show vulnerability in your relationships, acknowledging the fears that accompany each method. Understanding these fears is the first step in challenging and eventually overcoming them.

Instructions:

Step 1: Ways to Show Vulnerability

List three ways you can show vulnerability in a relationship. This could be through expressing your emotions, sharing personal stories, or asking for help.

Way 1:

_____

_____

Way 2:

_____

_____

Way 3:

_____

_____

Step 2: Associated Fears

For each method of showing vulnerability you've listed, identify the fear or fears that make you hesitant to take these steps.

Fear Associated with Way 1:

_____

_____

Fear Associated with Way 2:

_____

_____

Fear Associated with Way 3:

_____

_____

Step 3: Addressing the Fears

Reflect on strategies or steps you could take to address or mitigate these fears. Consider how understanding and facing these fears could lead to growth in your relationships.

Strategies to Address Fears:

_____

_____

_____

_____

_____

Outcome:

The goal of this exercise is to encourage you to explore different ways of being vulnerable in relationships, confronting the fears that prevent you from doing so. By identifying and planning to address these fears, you can work towards building stronger and more intimate connections.

Practical Exercise: Share a Personal Story to Practice Vulnerability

Objective:

This exercise aims to foster vulnerability by encouraging you to share a personal story or experience with someone you trust, but haven't opened up to about this particular aspect of your life. Sharing personal stories can deepen connections and encourage mutual openness.

Instructions:

1. **Choose the Story:** Reflect on personal experiences or stories you haven't shared with others before. Select one that feels significant to you and that you are comfortable sharing at this stage of your journey towards vulnerability.
2. **Select the Person:** Think of someone in your life with whom you feel safe and wish to deepen your connection—someone who has shown understanding and empathy towards you in the past.
3. **Share Your Story:** Find a quiet, comfortable time to share your story with this person. It could be during a walk, over a cup of coffee, or any setting that feels conducive to a heartfelt conversation.
4. **Observe and Reflect:** Pay attention to how you feel before, during, and after sharing your story. Note the reactions from the person you share it with and the dynamics of the conversation. Reflect on how this act of vulnerability affects your relationship.

Outcome:

By sharing a part of your personal history that you haven't before, you challenge yourself to be vulnerable in a safe environment. This can lead to strengthened bonds and a better understanding of the role vulnerability plays in building deeper connections.

Practical Exercise: Create a Ritual of Trust-Building

Objective:

The purpose of this exercise is to establish a ritual with a partner or close friend that encourages trust-building and ongoing vulnerability. Rituals can serve as a foundation for deepening emotional connections and reinforcing the security of the relationship.

Instructions:

1. **Develop the Ritual:** Together with your partner or friend, create a ritual that symbolizes trust and mutual support. This could be a weekly check-in where you both share your feelings and experiences from the week, a regular activity that encourages teamwork and communication, or simply a daily moment of gratitude shared between you.
2. **Implement the Ritual:** Commit to engaging in this ritual regularly. Make it a priority in your schedules and treat it as an important aspect of your relationship.
3. **Evaluate and Adapt:** After a period of practicing this ritual, reflect on its impact on your relationship. Discuss with your partner or friend what's working well and what might need adjustment. The goal is for the ritual to remain meaningful and supportive for both of you.

Outcome:

This exercise is designed to enhance the trust and emotional intimacy in your relationship through the establishment of a shared ritual. By committing to and valuing this ritual, you reinforce the importance of trust, support, and open communication in your connection.

Chapter 6

HEALING AND GROWTH

Most people who have avoidant attachment styles weren't abused or neglected. Their attachment style comes from learning to repress their emotions, which can be a result of many different scenarios. Perhaps you came from a large family where you didn't feel that your emotions were acknowledged, or you had a parent who was a narcissist that invalidated your emotions, or you may have been brought up to repress emotions. Or it's possible that abuse is the root cause for why you mask your emotions – if someone used your emotions to hurt you further, that will almost certainly result in you either becoming an avoidantly attached person or a disorganized attached person.

There are many situations that could create someone with this attachment style. Regardless of the why, it creates wounds that need to be healed so you can create secure attachments.

Identifying and Healing Attachment Wounds

The first part of healing wounds is to acknowledge that you have them. This is trying because it means being vulnerable. Avoiding attachments is literally a coping mechanism you learned as a child and it has created wounds that you need to address to heal them.

Up to this point, you've been working on self-reflection and being more aware of your emotions, and that is something you can start using as you start to address the root of your attachment style. As you understand why you react a certain way, you have to start questioning your negative thoughts about others. Sometimes people do deserve those negative thoughts, but for you, those thoughts are often automatic, and probably they aren't deserved. Even if they are deserved, you need to question why you feel negatively. You can use this to start understanding when someone deserves to be trusted and what they can do that proves they *don't* deserve to be trusted.

This isn't about constantly questioning yourself, but questioning the reason behind your thoughts. You may be fully justified, but you need to be sure of that, instead of just operating on an assumption that no one is trustworthy.

As you learn to question your initial thoughts, you will start to see when you can trust someone, and you can feel more secure with that person as a result. Using open communication and being more vulnerable with others will help you to start to heal, and that means questioning your own internal thoughts that are more reflexive than reflective.

Transforming Pain and Separation into Opportunities for Growth

There will be times when people prove that they can't be trusted – you aren't wrong to be wary. Whether you are facing new pain or pain from old wounds, you can learn to transform that pain into an opportunity to grow.

1. The more you start to acknowledge your emotions, the more active you should become in taking charge of those emotions. This can be questioning your initial negative thoughts, but it goes beyond that. When you realize you are feeling an emotion, own it, and understand why you are feeling it so that you can act on that emotion. In all honesty, that is the point of emotions – they are meant to let you know that you need something, to get you to react to them. When something causes you pain, you need to realize what it is that is hurting you. Historically, you have blamed others or being close to people as being why you hurt. The truth is far more complicated. It may be an action someone had that unintentionally hurt you – the proper reaction is to express that hurt to that person. That starts with acknowledging that you are hurt.

2. Understand the intention behind addressing that pain. Yes, there are cases where removing contact with someone may be the right solution. However, more often than not, the

intention to heal pain should be to address the problem, not avoid it. You aren't trying to avoid pain, but to address the root cause to see about changing things going forward.

3. Learn to start and reflect instead of immediately reacting. Your immediate reaction is to leave – and that isn't going to solve the problem. This may mean stopping and taking deep breaths to settle your nervous system first. Then you can let people know that you need some personal space to reflect. You need to confront the emotions, and that doesn't have to be done with other people present. However, it is important to let them know that you aren't simply avoiding it, you are working to process the pain.

4. Like failure, pain is always an opportunity to learn and improve yourself. There is a reason why you are feeling pain, and it may not be why you think. Take your painful experiences to understand more about yourself.

Over time, this will help you start to develop more reasonable boundaries that allow people to get closer while still helping you feel comfortable.

Self-Compassion and Self-Care

As someone who views emotions as weakness, self-compassion is virtually never a part of the avoidant attachment mentality. It is that lack of compassion that is shared with others, and why they think you are cold. The truth is that you don't have it toward anyone.

The point of self-compassion is to give yourself to feel emotions so that you can understand them. It's absolutely true that emotions can be entirely irrational, and that is absolutely frustrating. That doesn't change the fact that you feel them. Perhaps someone flirted with your partner, and you are jealous, even though you trust your partner. Instead of getting mad at yourself or your partner, face that jealousy and allow yourself to feel compassion for the part of you that is hurt. This kind of situation is going to be particularly triggering for you because you are already used to just leaving relationships at the first sign of trouble. If your partner isn't flirting back, they don't deserve to be punished for what someone else did. By being compassionate toward yourself, you will be better able to express your discomfort to the situation. A good partner will then ensure that if this happens again in the future, they will shut down the flirting.

When you recognize that you are allowed to have emotions and learn to be compassionate to yourself, you will be a much better communicator with other people. That connection to your emotions means you have a better understanding of the situation, the cause, and what might help to alleviate the pain.

Seeking Support and Therapy

Asking for help is definitely not in your wheelhouse. For a lot of people with this attachment style there is almost a pride in being able to handle things on their own. If you are going to change, then you need help. Since you have trouble trusting people, that is a pretty big ask.

Finding a good therapist is often a very good move. The person clearly has a motive to help you, and they are an outside party to your relationships. There are therapists who specialize in helping people with this attachment style, so if you feel that you need someone you think is more trustworthy, they likely have the tools to help you feel more comfortable and confident in your care.

A therapist can offer a safe space and place for you to start exploring and understanding your emotions. Their motivations are clear, so you are not likely to question their motives. You may think they are wrong, but they will already have the knowledge for how to work with you to express why you think they are wrong. There is a push and pull that you can develop with a therapist that can be less clear with people in your personal life. It is a bit like practicing how to be vulnerable when the stakes feel much lower. Your relationship with a therapist is more transactional, and it is unlikely that the therapist is going to reject you, removing a lot of the reasons for concern that causes you to avoid others. That alone can help you start to safely explore things that you have ignored and avoided for years.

Exercise: Write a Letter of Forgiveness to Yourself for Past Relationship Mistakes

Objective:

This exercise encourages self-forgiveness for past mistakes or missteps in relationships. Recognizing and forgiving yourself for these can be a crucial step in healing and moving forward towards healthier relationships.

Instructions:

Step 1: Reflect on Mistakes

Think about past relationships where you believe you made mistakes or wish you had acted differently. Choose one or two instances that stand out to you.

Mistake 1:

_____

_____

Mistake 2:

_____

_____

Step 2: Draft Your Letter

Write a letter to yourself expressing forgiveness for these mistakes. Acknowledge what happened, how it made you feel, and why you forgive yourself. Remember, the goal is not to dwell on guilt but to recognize your humanity and capacity for growth.

Letter Draft:

_____

_____

_____

_____

_____

Step 3: Affirm Your Growth

Conclude your letter with affirmations of growth and how you intend to use these experiences to better yourself and your future relationships. Emphasize the lessons learned and the steps you're taking towards emotional growth.

Affirmations of Growth:

_____

_____

_____

_____

_____

Outcome:

Completing this exercise aims to foster a sense of self-compassion and forgiveness, essential components of healing and growth. By acknowledging past mistakes and forgiving yourself, you open the door to more mindful and compassionate relationship dynamics in the future.

Exercise: Create a Self-Care Plan That Addresses Emotional, Physical, and Mental Health

Objective:

This exercise is designed to help you develop a holistic self-care plan that nurtures your emotional, physical, and mental health. Taking care of all aspects of yourself is vital for overall well-being and forms the foundation of building healthy relationships with others.

Instructions:

Step 1: Emotional Self-Care Activities

List activities or practices that support your emotional well-being. These could include journaling, therapy sessions, or engaging in hobbies that bring you joy.

Emotional Self-Care Activities:

_____

_____

_____

_____

_____

Step 2: Physical Self-Care Activities

Identify actions you can take to support your physical health. This might involve regular exercise, nutritious eating, or ensuring you get enough sleep.

Physical Self-Care Activities:

_____

_____

_____

_____

_____

Step 3: Mental Self-Care Activities

Consider practices that contribute to your mental health, such as mindfulness, reading, or learning something new.

Mental Self-Care Activities:

_____

_____

_____

_____

_____

Outcome:

By creating a balanced self-care plan, you aim to nurture your well-being across all areas of your life. This holistic approach to self-care not only improves your health and happiness but also strengthens your capacity for forming and maintaining healthy relationships.

Practical Exercise: Attend a Therapy Session or Support Group Meeting Focusing on Attachment Issues

Objective:

This exercise aims to provide you with professional insight and peer support in addressing attachment issues. Attending a therapy session or a support group meeting can help you understand your attachment style better and learn strategies for forming healthier relationships.

Instructions:

1. **Research and Select:** Look for a therapist who specializes in attachment theory or find a support group meeting that focuses on attachment issues. Online platforms can offer virtual options if in-person meetings are not feasible.
2. **Attend the Session:** Go into the session with an open mind. Be prepared to listen, share your experiences if you're comfortable, and learn from others' insights.
3. **Reflect:** After the session, take some time to reflect on what you learned. Consider how the insights gained might apply to your own experiences with attachment and relationships.

Outcome:

Attending a therapy session or support group meeting on attachment issues aims to enhance your understanding of your own attachment style and provide strategies for overcoming challenges related to it. Engaging with others facing similar issues can also offer a sense of community and support.

Practical Exercise: Implement One Self-Care Activity Daily for a Week and Journal the Effects

Objective:

The purpose of this exercise is to emphasize the importance of self-care in improving your overall well-being and how it impacts your ability to form and maintain healthy relationships. By dedicating time to self-care daily and reflecting on its effects, you can better understand its role in your life.

Instructions:

1. **Choose a Self-Care Activity:** Select a self-care activity that you can realistically commit to doing every day for a week. This could be anything from exercise, meditation, journaling, to spending time on a hobby.

2. **Daily Implementation:** Dedicate time each day to engage in your chosen self-care activity. Try to do it at the same time each day to build a routine.

3. **Journal the Effects:** After each self-care session, journal about how you feel immediately afterward and any long-term effects you notice over the week. Pay attention to changes in your mood, energy levels, and how you interact with others.

Outcome:

This exercise is designed to highlight the benefits of regular self-care on your emotional, physical, and mental health. By journaling the effects, you aim to gain insights into how self-care practices influence your well-being and relationships, encouraging you to make them a consistent part of your life.

Chapter 7

FROM AVOIDANT TO SECURE ATTACHMENT

No matter how impossible it may seem, it is never too late to learn how to develop secure attachments with the people in your life. All of the running you've done from relationships in the past can come to an end, and you can start treating people as individuals. Because up to this point, you've been treating everyone the same – when you question their motivations, it's easier to just leave.

You can't change your childhood, but you can start to heal the child within you who has made it so much more difficult to have meaningful relationships. As a result, you can finally have the kind of relationship the child wants.

The Evolution from Avoidant to Secure Attachment: Processes and Practices

Every attachment style can be changed. Someone with a secure attachment can get into an abusive relationship and change to any of the other relationships. Someone who has an insecure attachment can learn to foster secure attachments. It is a long process, but it is worth it. Attachment styles aren't disorders or personality traits. They are simply how you form (or avoid) connections with others.

We've already gone through a number of the steps, so you are already working toward shifting your attachment style. The following is the full process, as well as things you can practice to work on each step along the way.

1. Work on self-awareness. There are so many excuses you have for avoiding real relationships, such as you have met the right person and people are trustworthy. You need to understand what your reasons are so that you can start questioning and dismantling these ideas. By reflecting on your day in your evening, you can begin to see where you have been using these fallacies to justify avoiding any kind of real relationship.

2. Identify and understand your deactivation strategies. You must learn to be honest with yourself because if you aren't, you won't be able to move past this stage. What is it that you do that creates space between you and the people in your life, and why do you do that? When you start to get to know someone, you probably initially feel excited. What is it that made you decide that you needed to step back from that experience? Is it something they did, or something you found to be a "flaw" that justified backing off? Perhaps there was a real red flag, and your reaction is logical. More often than not though, the problem was likely a small flaw that can be addressed with an open conversation. You may find that the person is grateful for your being open, and you could find that you are happy that you did. Especially if it helps you feel closer to them.

3. Start working on learning to learn how to seek support. A therapist can be a good start, but they aren't going to be the final solution to avoidant attachment. You can start small and build up trust. This does not mean you have to entirely give up your autonomy – there are plenty of things that are one-person jobs. However, your life isn't full of things that only you can and should do. There are going to be times when getting help is a much better idea. For example, if you are moving, have a large project, or want to learn a new skill, there are probably people in your life you can help. Similarly, don't look down on people who ask you for help. It can be a big compliment for someone to ask you for help. This is a chance to bond with someone as you are working toward the same goal.

4. Record the things that you appreciate in your relationships. This is something you can do on your own, especially in the beginning. You need to learn to be aware of the things you enjoy and love about your relationships. If you have a romantic partner who makes you feel interested and enjoys things you enjoy, this is a lot more important than some small flaw. By knowing what it is that you enjoy about being with someone, it is much harder for those little things to seem like a good enough reason to withdraw from the relationship. You are primed to look for the negatives; take the time to find the positives, and you will probably see that they vastly outweigh the negatives. It also means recognizing the value that people add to your life, and things you may lose by avoiding those relationships.

5. Work toward managing conflict, instead of entirely avoiding it. If you are feeling particularly triggered or stressed, you can ask for some time to process conflict, but it should not become

a way to entirely avoid the conflict. Arter you have taken some time to calm down, you need to go back and have a hard conversation. It will be uncomfortable, and it could have a bad result, but at least it will be a learning experience. There is also a very good chance that communicating your emotions and outlook will create a deeper bond. Yes, the relationship may end up changing as a result of the discussion, but even that is better than simply dropping the relationship without having tried. Over time, you will get more comfortable with this approach. Also, be aware that dealing with conflict is difficult for everyone, not just you. By its nature, conflict brings up negative emotions, but that means it is an opportunity to start working on compromises and better understanding the other side.

This seems like a short list, but each step can take weeks, months, or even years. You are working to overcome an ingrained way of dealing with people, and it isn't going to be something you can easily change.

Cultivating Secure Relationships: Strategies for Individuals and Couples

There is a wealth of advice out there for helping an avoidant attached person to learn to feel comfortable with opening up and being vulnerable. Most of it can be boiled down to a few key things.

1. Be patient with them. They are going to have times when they shut down and need space. Don't push them because that will continue to push them further away. Give them time to process, but let them know that you are there when they are ready.

2. Create a space that feels safe for them. This doesn't need to be a single place, but more an environment where they can start to be comfortable opening up to you. One of the best ways to do that is to let your partner know that you accept who they are and that you are there to help. Just that permission to accept themselves can help them to feel that you are a safe person.

3. Realize they don't have the same outlook on needs as you. They see needs as being something they can always handle on their own. When you ask for help, it demonstrates

that it is safe to ask for help, although it may be confusing to them in the beginning. They aren't used to asking for help, so you can help to show them the kinds of situations where help may not be necessary, but it is greatly appreciated.

4. Don't try to control their reactions or behaviors. They may simply walk away. Let them. They may be on the verge of a panic attack or they may be experiencing high stress levels, and they need to get themselves under control. You being present isn't going to help. By trying to control their reactions and behaviors, you are playing into the perception that you have motives to the relationship that they may not know. By letting them manage themselves for now, you are reinforcing that you are a safe space for them to be themselves.

5. Give them their time alone. This is going to be really difficult if you have an anxious attachment style, but you have to do it. These are people who are used to dealing with things on their own, so they need more time to themselves to manage their emotions, especially in the early days. Even after a few years, they will need to have time alone to properly handle how they are feeling, and you can't expect that you are going to be the solution. You may be able to help them work through it, but they have to do some of the work on their own.

6. Encourage and practice open, honest communication. Be very clear about what you feel and what your words mean.

7. Realize that when they reject you, it's not personal. Or at least it is rarely a person. It's a defense mechanism that they are working to overcome.

8. Try to be calm when you engage in conversations, especially ones that involve conflict. The higher the emotions, the more likely they are to shut down and leave.

9. Be careful with criticism because these are seen as personal attacks, even if you didn't mean it that way. Instead of being critical or complaining about them, state your feelings as a request.

It can be really hard to work with someone who is avoidantly attached because their attachment to you is much more tenuous. However, they can make great partners because they can keep a level head and get things done. By helping them to work on feeling safe to have and express emotions, you will be able to better understand and support them.

The Transmission of Avoidant Attachment from Parent to Child and How to Build Secure Attachments

Children developing an avoidant attachment style can come from many different situations, and usually it isn't intentional. Parents often mean well or aren't aware that what they are doing is teaching their children to repress their emotions in a way that means they won't be willing to form deeper relationships. There is no one single type of relationship that will result in an avoidant attachment. A family may have four children, each with their own attachment style that reflects how they were treated within the family.

The following are the kinds of behaviors towards infants and children that are more likely to cause them to learn to have an avoidant attachment style.

- Leaving a child to cry instead of acknowledging the problem. There was a long-standing myth that children should be allowed to cry because they were "manipulating" their parents into holding them more or giving them more attention. When an infant cries, they are doing so because they can't state what they need. They are manipulating anyone – it's the only means of communication that they have. The problem may not be obvious, but the infant needs your attention, even if it is to alleviate a fear or distress.
- Telling a child to "suck it up," "to be quiet," or to "stop crying." Anything that indicates the child should not express emotions is teaching that child not to express any emotions. Yes, there are times and spaces when a child may need to be quiet, but it should not be something constant in their lives. Learn to listen to your child because their needs should be met, not repressed. When a child acts up, there is almost always a deeper reason for it, so you should be paying attention and figuring out why they are acting out.
- Shaming a child for having or expressing emotions. This is like the last one. Instead of making your child feel ashamed, you need to learn to listen to them and to try to help them learn to manage those emotions. This is not only healthier for them, it will make your life a lot easier in the long run as they reach their teenage years and adulthood as they will be much better adjusted to life.
- Walking away or ignoring children when they are upset or are showing emotions. Yes, there will be times when you may need to step away for a minute or two because you are feeling stressed and you need to calm down first. That is fine. However, you need to return and address those emotions. Work to comfort them and talk through what they are feeling. Toddlers may not have a big vocabulary, but you can almost certainly help them through their concerns because they are so much simpler than what upsets an adult.

- Expecting your child to be emotionally independent from you. This should have to some extent over time, but it should not happen when your child is young. Even during their teenage years, they need emotional support. Don't expect them to start acting like adults and managing their emotions when they are young because they aren't equipped to do that yet. You need to help them learn how to do that, just like you teach them how to ride a bike or swim.

- Expressing a lot of emotion to the point where it largely overshadows their own. Children learn to shrink themselves when they are around really emotional parents. While you should express healthy emotions with your child, it should not be done to the point where you ignore your child's emotions.

It is actually quite easy to teach a child to have an avoidant attachment style because it is done unintentionally. Unlike the other insecure attachment styles, this is often a result of trying to do the right thing, but doing it in a way that means avoiding emotions. Children need to have emotional support just as much as they need to have any other type of support. That is what helps them to develop a secure attachment style.

Exercise: Journal About the Changes You Wish to See in Your Attachment Style

Objective:

This exercise aims to help you reflect on and articulate the specific changes you wish to see in your attachment style. Recognizing these desired changes is the first step towards working on them and fostering secure attachments.

Instructions:

Step 1: Reflect on Current State

Consider your current attachment style and its characteristics. Think about how it manifests in your relationships and the impact it has on your connections with others.

Current Attachment Style Characteristics:

_____

_____

_____

_____

_____

Step 2: Desired Changes

Identify and list the changes you wish to see in your attachment style. Be specific about how you want your interactions and relationships to evolve.

Desired Changes:

_____

_____

_____

_____

_____

Step 3: Visualize the Outcome

Imagine how your relationships and daily interactions would look with these changes in place. Reflect on the positive outcomes and feelings associated with adopting a more secure attachment style.

Visualization of Outcomes:

_____

_____

_____

_____

_____

Outcome:

By completing this exercise, you will have a clearer understanding of the specific changes you aim to make in your attachment style. This clarity can guide your actions and choices in relationships, steering you towards more secure and fulfilling connections.

Exercise: Write a Plan for Addressing Avoidant Behaviors in Your Relationships

Objective:

The purpose of this exercise is to create a structured plan to address and modify avoidant behaviors in your relationships. Having a concrete plan can help you take actionable steps towards forming more secure attachments.

Instructions:

Step 1: Identify Avoidant Behaviors

List the avoidant behaviors you recognize in yourself that you wish to change. Be honest about the actions or patterns that hinder deeper connections in your relationships.

Avoidant Behaviors:

_____

_____

_____

_____

Step 2: Strategies for Change

For each behavior listed, write a strategy or action plan to address and alter that behavior. Consider techniques such as mindfulness, communication exercises, or seeking support from a therapist.

Strategies for Change:

_____

_____

_____

_____

Step 3: Set Goals and Timelines

Set realistic goals for implementing these strategies, along with timelines. Having specific goals and timelines can help you stay on track and measure your progress in modifying avoidant behaviors.

Goals and Timelines:

_____

_____

_____

_____

_____

Outcome:

This exercise is designed to equip you with a personalized plan to tackle avoidant behaviors, promoting growth towards a secure attachment style. By actively working on these strategies, you can improve your ability to form and maintain deeper, more meaningful relationships.

Practical Exercise: Practice a New Attachment-Focused Behavior with a Partner or Child

Objective:

This exercise encourages the application of a new behavior aimed at fostering secure attachment in an existing relationship with a partner or child. By introducing and consistently practicing a new behavior, you can work towards altering patterns of avoidance and enhancing emotional connectivity.

Instructions:

1. **Select a Behavior:** Choose a specific behavior to implement that promotes secure attachment. This could be anything from initiating more physical affection, actively engaging in daily conversations about feelings and experiences, to setting aside regular quality time together.
2. **Implement the Behavior:** Begin integrating this behavior into your daily interactions with your partner or child. Make a conscious effort to be consistent and genuine in your approach, ensuring that the behavior aligns with the needs and comfort levels of both you and your loved one.
3. **Observe and Reflect:** Pay attention to how this new behavior impacts your relationship. Notice any changes in the emotional atmosphere, communication patterns, or the overall bond between you and your partner or child. Reflect on how this practice influences your feelings towards attachment and intimacy.

Outcome:

The aim of this exercise is to directly experience the positive effects of secure attachment behaviors on your relationships. Through consistent practice, you can learn to overcome avoidant tendencies, fostering stronger, more emotionally connected relationships.

Practical Exercise: Teach Someone About Attachment Theory and Discuss Its Relevance to Your Relationship

Objective:

This exercise involves educating a partner, family member, or friend about attachment theory and exploring together how it applies to your relationship. Discussing attachment theory can enhance mutual understanding and encourage both parties to work on building a more secure attachment.

Instructions:

1. **Prepare:** Gather information on attachment theory that you find insightful and relevant to your relationship. Focus on aspects that resonate with your experiences and those of the person you're discussing this with.
2. **Engage in Discussion:** Share what you've learned about attachment theory with your partner, family member, or friend. Explain how you see aspects of attachment theory playing out in your own relationship dynamics.
3. **Reflect and Plan:** Together, reflect on the insights gained from the discussion. Identify specific behaviors or patterns you both agree to work on to foster a more secure attachment in your relationship. Set actionable goals and consider how you can support each other in this process.

Outcome:

By educating someone close to you about attachment theory and discussing its relevance to your relationship, this exercise aims to open up new avenues for understanding and empathy. Through shared knowledge and a mutual commitment to growth, you can collaboratively work towards nurturing a more secure and fulfilling relationship.

Chapter 8

NURTURING
EMOTIONAL RESILIENCE

People are aware of what they need to do to be physically healthy, even if they fail to actually follow through. Over the last decade or two, there has been a lot greater emphasis on people learning to be aware of how they feel emotionally, so there has been a lot of attention going toward mental health. What most people overlook though is the need to be emotionally healthy. Much of how a person deals with emotions is based on how they learn to deal with emotions when they are children. Attachment style is only one aspect of emotional management.

No matter how you were raised, you can learn to be emotionally resilient as an adult. Like learning a language, it is going to take a lot of work initially. Once you start to learn what you need to do, you will find it easier to start reprogramming your reactions to emotions to be able to express them in a way that is healthier and more productive.

Countering Negative Thought Patterns

As someone with an avoidant attachment, you tend to think more negatively than positively. Since you rely so heavily on yourself, you are much more likely to perpetuate that way of thinking. Disrupting the constant stream of negative thoughts about the world is part of why you need to be mindful of how you think. The more you notice how you think, the more you will see the negative thread that tends to flow through most of it.

Countering negative thoughts with something more positive, or at least something that is probably more realistic, is necessary to start developing emotional resilience. Studies have shown that optimistic people tend to live longer, they have a better quality of life, and they are more likely to overcome diseases than pessimists. Since you tend to ignore your emotions, and you have a more negative look at this natural reaction to the world around you, you have to learn how to notice when your thinking is focusing on the negative. You need to pay attention to when you are thinking negatively about yourself or your emotions so that you can retrain how you think about yourself and your emotions.

Once you start to realize you are having negative thoughts about yourself or your emotions, you can begin to practice self-compassion.

Over time, this should start to extend to your negative thoughts about other people. Instead of assuming that someone is going to hurt you, you can interrupt the assumption by reminding yourself that it is no more than that. An assumption based on little to no evidence. If the assumption is based on past experiences with that specific person, you may be right, and then you should continue to be protective of yourself. You can also see about reaching an understanding with that person. Perhaps they are having a negative reaction to how you previously treated them.

All of this requires that you realize when you are thinking negatively, then countering that thought process with something that is much more closely aligned with reality, instead of a pessimistic perspective.

Building Emotional Resilience

This is something that you can begin working on in the beginning, but it is something that you are probably going to be refining over the rest of your life. There will be times when your emotions will become too intense, when you won't be able to manage them. That is why having deeper connections can be incredibly helpful. However, you can start to work on your own emotional resilience so that you aren't entirely reliant on others to help you through the inevitably emotionally trying times.

1. Counter negative thoughts with more optimistic thinking.
2. Deal with your fears instead of ignoring them. The more you avoid your fears, the more intense they become, and they can get to the point where you become unable to react when you are confronted with your fears.
3. Stick to your moral compass. We all have a moral compass, but over time many people learn to compromise that compass. And when we do, it creates a lot of negative emotions, particularly regret and shame. If you learn what your moral compass is, you need to make

sure that you don't compromise those morals. As someone who is avoidant attached, this is probably a lot easier for you to do, but you need to keep it in mind as you start forming attachments to others.

4. Develop a social support network. This is one of the biggest benefits of having a support network. They are able to help you through the emotionally rough times, and help you ensure that you don't get into a really dark place.

5. Take the time to be physically active every day. Exercise can help you stay in shape, but it is also one of the best tools to resetting and managing emotions. Physical activity helps to calm emotions and can work out a lot of negative emotions. Being active also releases some chemicals in your brain that boost positive thinking and emotions, making it a great way to manage your emotional health, along with your physical and mental health.

6. Engage in brain games. There are plenty on your phone that can help you keep your brain active. Thoughts are a big part of what shapes emotions, and this is why things like OCD can be so detrimental. When a person starts to focus on one thing to the point that their thoughts spiral, it can have not only a mental effect, but a very negative emotional effect. Brain games can help you keep your thinking clearer, as well as being a nice way of spending 10 to 15 minutes of your day. Like exercise, working your brain is likely to have a very positive effect on all aspects of your health.

7. Learn to be more cognitively flexible. This doesn't mean that you should compromise your morals, but you shouldn't have a rigid way of thinking. To deal with stressful situations, it's best to be able to look at situations from multiple angles. This is similar to how your brain works when you are problem solving. By being more mentally flexible, you will be able to start seeing the good through the bad and to develop healthier coping mechanisms.

Emotional resilience requires working on your physical and mental health just as much as it means learning to manage your emotions. That's because no one aspect of yourself can be isolated and treated. By taking a more holistic approach, you will find that emotional resilience is much easier to achieve.

Cultivating Healthy Relationships

As someone who is not accustomed to cultivating healthy relationships, there is a lot that may seem obvious to most people that is less obvious to you. There is a lot to do if you want to grow positive relationships with others, but we have already covered most of them.

The following is a list of things you should do to help cultivate the kinds of relationships that will help you to better manage your emotions, or to have a support network who is able to help you.

1. Learn to communicate.
2. Don't be afraid to be honest, but don't be blunt or cruel as you are honest with others.
3. Develop healthy boundaries, not boundaries that exclude everyone.
4. Learn to be an active listener.
5. Practice empathy.
6. Open up about what you enjoy and discuss shared interests.
7. Express your appreciation to others.
8. Make dedicated time for people close to you, especially romantic partners.
9. Understand that you aren't going to agree about everything, so find common ground.

By working on these, you will find that you can start to open up and be more engaged in your relationships. Cultivating healthy relationships is good not only for developing a support network, it teaches you to better connect with and understand your emotions.

Enhancing Emotional Intelligence

Emotional intelligence is something you can acquire, no matter how old you are. It refers to your ability to identify and manage your emotions, as well as those of the people around you. Empathy shows that you are able to apply emotional intelligence to others as you can understand their situation because of your own experiences.

Again, we've covered most of these already. As you start to develop deeper relationships, it's important to continue to develop your emotional intelligence.

1. Be self-aware.
2. Learn cues that help you understand how others feel.
3. Be an active listener.
4. Communicate clearly with other people.
5. Practice positive thinking.
6. Be more empathetic toward others.
7. Work toward being open-minded so you can stand other people's perspectives.
8. Learn how to accept feedback without getting defensive or thinking negatively about the person delivering the feedback.
9. Learn how to be calm when you start to feel stress. Another way to think about this is to learn how to manage stress so that you don't lash out emotionally.

This is going to take a lot of time and practice, no matter your attachment style. Emotional intelligence today does not get nearly enough attention, so it is something that we should all work to improve.

Exercise: Identify and Challenge One Negative Thought Pattern You Have About Relationships

Objective:

This exercise aims to help you recognize and confront a negative thought pattern you have regarding relationships, facilitating a shift towards a more positive and constructive mindset.

Instructions:

Step 1: Identify the Negative Thought Pattern

Reflect on your thoughts about relationships and identify one negative pattern that frequently occurs. This could be a belief that you are not worthy of love, that all relationships end in hurt, or that showing vulnerability is a weakness.

Negative Thought Pattern:

_____

_____

_____

_____

_____

Step 2: Challenge the Pattern

Once you have identified the negative thought pattern, challenge it. Ask yourself whether it's based on factual evidence or past experiences that may not dictate future outcomes. Consider alternative, more positive perspectives.

Challenge to the Pattern:

_____

_____

_____

_____

_____

Step 3: Create a Positive Counterstatement

Develop a positive counterstatement to your negative thought pattern. This statement should reflect a more optimistic and realistic viewpoint on relationships.

Positive Counterstatement:

_____

_____

_____

_____

_____

Outcome:

Completing this exercise will help you to begin dismantling harmful thought patterns about relationships, paving the way for a more positive approach to forming and maintaining connections.

Exercise: Develop a List of Qualities You Seek in Healthy Relationships

Objective:

The goal of this exercise is to articulate the qualities and characteristics you value and seek in healthy relationships. This clarity can guide your efforts in building and nurturing more fulfilling connections.

Instructions:

Step 1: Reflect on Desired Qualities

Think about your past relationships and what qualities contributed to a sense of fulfillment and happiness. Also, consider what was lacking and how it impacted your connection. List the qualities you believe are essential in a healthy relationship.

Desired Qualities:

_____

_____

_____

_____

_____

Step 2: Prioritize the List

Review the list of qualities you've compiled and prioritize them. Identify which ones are non-negotiable for you and which ones you might be more flexible about.

Prioritized Qualities:

_____

_____

_____

_____

_____

Step 3: Plan to Seek and Foster These Qualities

Create a plan on how you will seek these qualities in future relationships and how you can also cultivate these qualities within yourself. This might involve setting personal development goals or strategies for engaging with potential partners.

Plan of Action:

_____

_____

_____

_____

_____

Outcome:

By identifying and prioritizing the qualities you value in relationships, this exercise helps you focus on what truly matters to you in connections with others. It also encourages personal growth as you strive to embody these qualities.

Practical Exercise: Practice a Daily Emotional Intelligence Exercise

Objective:

Enhance your emotional intelligence by practicing daily exercises that involve identifying, naming, and exploring your feelings. This exercise aims to improve your self-awareness and emotional regulation, key components of emotional intelligence.

Instructions:

1. **Set Aside Time Each Day:** Dedicate a few minutes each day to focus on your emotional state. It could be in the morning, during a break, or before bed.
2. **Identify and Name Your Feelings:** During this time, reflect on how you are feeling at that moment. Try to be as specific as possible in naming your emotions, going beyond basic labels like "happy" or "sad" to more nuanced feelings like "content," "anxious," or "frustrated."
3. **Explore the Emotion:** Once you've identified and named your emotion, spend a moment reflecting on what might be causing this feeling. Consider any events, interactions, or thoughts that could have contributed to this emotional state.

Outcome:

By consistently practicing this exercise, you aim to become more attuned to your emotions and the triggers behind them. This heightened awareness can lead to better emotional regulation and improved relationships, as you become more capable of expressing your feelings in a constructive manner.

Practical Exercise: Adapt a New Coping Strategy for Stress

Objective:

Implement a new strategy to cope with stress and observe its effects on your emotional well-being and relationships. The goal is to find healthier ways to deal with stress that do not involve avoidance and can positively impact your connections with others.

Instructions:

1. **Choose a New Coping Strategy:** Select a stress management technique that you have not tried before or have not consistently implemented. This could be mindfulness meditation, exercise, journaling, or engaging in a hobby.
2. **Implement the Strategy:** Commit to using this coping strategy every time you feel stressed for a period (e.g., two weeks). Make a note of each instance you use the strategy and any immediate effects you notice on your stress levels.
3. **Reflect on Its Impact:** After the trial period, reflect on how this new coping strategy has affected your stress levels and your relationships. Consider whether you've been more present and engaged in your interactions and if your stress has been less likely to negatively impact those around you.

Outcome:

The aim of this exercise is to find effective, healthy ways to manage stress, thereby improving your own emotional resilience and the quality of your relationships. By adopting new coping strategies, you can reduce the likelihood of stress leading to avoidance and disconnection, fostering stronger, more supportive connections instead.

Chapter 9

ADVANCED STRATEGIES FOR RELATIONSHIP ENHANCEMENT

As you learn to develop your relationships, you will start to feel more comfortable and confident with dealing with your emotions and your relationships. However, you may reach a point where you feel that you are stuck and unable to continue to grow relationships. This chapter will help you to learn how to continue to improve and grow your relationships.

Conflict Resolution Techniques

So far we haven't gone into as much detail about conflict resolution, and that's because it is going to take the most work to master. It's something that everyone can work on because it doesn't take much for conflicts to go very wrong impossibly quickly. The great thing is that you can apply these to every situation, not just your close, personal relationships.

1. Take the time to define the problem and where the conflict arises.
2. Begin open communication and ensure people understand that it is a place where people should feel safe.
3. Establish common ground.
4. Set a goal and regularly evaluate the situation to see how you are progressing toward that goal. This could include establishing metrics for things like work where you can see how things are shaping up and where more work is required.
5. Develop a plan of action.

6. Provide regular feedback. Make sure that this includes the positives and the negatives. You should never focus on just one aspect because there will be areas where the progress is good, and areas where more work is required.

Good communication is absolutely essential to every step and strategy to resolving conflict. If you feel yourself getting emotional, take a step back. If you notice others starting to get upset, have them step back. Intense emotions should be avoided as much as possible for the conflict to find a resolution that is more likely to work for everyone.

Applying Attachment Theory to Personal Growth

According to the Attachment Theory, a secure attachment will facilitate improved personal growth. Ironically, it is a belief in free will that tends to make personal growth possible. People who are avoidantly attached benefit from focusing on a person's free will. This is because they tend to think that no one can be trusted, so there is no point in trying. By rephrasing that thought process as they have the ability to open up and see if people are trustworthy, they find it easier to do. This then allows them to start pursuing personal growth in their lives.

The reason this works is because their normal way of looking at people is that there is already a decided result in how the relationships will play out. By realizing that they actually have more control over the end result of the relationship, or at least just as much say in how things will play out, it is easier to see that there are multiple potential outcomes. The relationship may not work out in the end, but it can have a very different conclusion. It's also more likely to have a better outcome than what they used to anticipate.

Identifying and Processing Attachment Trauma

We've looked at healing old emotional wounds and how you treat children can create the same kind of insecure attachment. Now it's time to start digging into attachment trauma, something that might be best if you talk to your therapist. However, these are the points that can help you as you learn more about yourself, your emotions, and why you've been avoiding closer relationships.

Attachment trauma occurs when the bonding process between you and your parents or caregivers is disrupted. This creates a sense of distress that you tend to hold onto for the rest of your life if you don't actively work to change it. Usually attachment trauma occurs repeatedly over the years, creating a much more complex trauma that reinforces your attachment style.

Unfortunately, there is a physical aspect to this trauma, even if there is no physical abuse. That's because stress causes stress, and we have a physical reaction to stress. The most natural is the fight or flight response, which has been updated to include the freeze response. For someone who is avoidantly attached, the freeze response isn't used. Your experience is a need to either fight the situation or flee. As a result you leave since you aren't likely to be able to deal with conflict. People who are anxiously attached are the ones who tend to experience a freeze reaction to these kinds of stressors.

It is best to discuss your own personal experiences with your therapists. This does mean being vulnerable and reliving the things that caused you the pain. That is why you should be doing it in a safe space with someone who can help you to process it. Thinking about and reliving the trauma that caused your current attachment style will create a physical reaction that can be unhealthy. A professional can help you navigate the pain and stress to reach a place of acceptance and healing.

Exercise: Write a Conflict Resolution Plan for a Recurring Issue in a Relationship

Objective:

This exercise is designed to help you construct a plan to address and resolve a recurring conflict in one of your relationships, using strategic and thoughtful approaches to conflict resolution.

Instructions:

Step 1: Identify the Recurring Issue

Reflect on your relationships and identify a specific conflict that keeps arising. Describe the issue clearly and objectively, focusing on the behaviors or circumstances that contribute to the conflict.

Recurring Issue:

_____

_____

_____

_____

_____

Step 2: Develop Resolution Strategies

Outline strategies that you believe could address the root cause of the issue. Consider approaches like open communication, setting clear expectations, and seeking mutual understanding.

Resolution Strategies:

_____

_____

_____

_____

_____

Step 3: Plan for Implementation and Feedback

Create a step-by-step plan for implementing your resolution strategies, including how you will introduce the plan to the other person involved. Also, think about how you will gather feedback on the effectiveness of the resolution process.

Implementation and Feedback Plan:

_____

_____

_____

_____

_____

Outcome:

The goal of this exercise is to equip you with a practical and actionable plan to tackle a recurring conflict, fostering healthier and more constructive communication. By approaching the issue with a clear strategy, you aim to not only resolve the immediate conflict but also to strengthen the overall relationship.

Exercise: Reflect on How Attachment Theory Has Influenced Your View of Personal Growth

Objective:

This exercise encourages you to reflect on the impact of attachment theory on your understanding of personal growth, particularly in how secure attachments can facilitate or hinder your development.

Instructions:

Step 1: Understand Attachment Theory's Impact

Think about what you've learned about attachment theory and how it applies to your life. Consider how your attachment style may have influenced your behaviors, relationships, and personal growth.

Impact of Attachment Theory:

_____

_____

_____

_____

_____

Step 2: Identify Areas for Growth

Based on your understanding of attachment theory, identify specific areas in your personal growth that have been affected by your attachment style. This could include trust in relationships, openness to new experiences, or dealing with emotions.

Areas for Growth:

_____

_____

_____

_____

_____

Step 3: Plan for Application

Create a plan for how you can use insights from attachment theory to address and improve these areas of personal growth. Include specific actions you can take and how you will measure progress.

Application Plan:

_____

_____

_____

_____

_____

Outcome:

By completing this exercise, you aim to gain a deeper understanding of how your attachment style impacts your personal growth. The reflection and planning process should help you identify practical steps to use attachment theory as a tool for enhancing your development and enriching your relationships.

Practical Exercise 1: Implement a Conflict Resolution Technique in a Real-Life Disagreement

Objective:

This exercise aims to apply a conflict resolution technique to a real-life disagreement, allowing you to practice and refine your skills in navigating conflicts more effectively and constructively.

Instructions:

1. **Prepare:** Before entering into a discussion where you anticipate disagreement, choose a conflict resolution technique you've learned about, such as active listening, identifying underlying needs, or finding common ground. Briefly review the steps involved in this technique.

2. **Apply the Technique:** During the disagreement, consciously apply the chosen conflict resolution technique. Focus on maintaining open communication, respect, and a willingness to understand the other person's perspective.

3. **Reflect:** After the disagreement, reflect on the experience. Consider what went well, what could have been improved, and how the conflict resolution technique influenced the outcome of the disagreement.

Outcome:

The purpose of this exercise is to practice applying conflict resolution techniques in real-life situations, enhancing your ability to navigate disagreements constructively. By reflecting on the experience, you can identify areas for improvement and further develop your conflict resolution skills.

Practical Exercise: Engage in an Activity That Helps Process Past Trauma, Such as Art Therapy or Journaling

Objective:

This exercise encourages you to engage in a therapeutic activity that can help you process and heal from past trauma. Activities like art therapy and journaling offer a creative and expressive outlet for exploring your feelings and experiences.

Instructions:

1. **Choose an Activity:** Select an activity that resonates with you as a means of processing emotions. This could be art therapy, where you express your feelings through drawing, painting, or sculpting, or journaling, where you write about your experiences and emotions.

2. **Engage Regularly:** Dedicate time to regularly engage in your chosen activity. Set aside a quiet, private space where you can focus on your self-expression without interruptions.

3. **Reflect on the Experience:** After each session, take a moment to reflect on what the activity brought up for you. Consider any insights gained, emotions processed, or relief experienced through this expressive work.

Outcome:

The aim of this exercise is to provide you with a therapeutic tool for processing past trauma, fostering emotional healing and growth. Through regular engagement and reflection, you can gain deeper insights into your experiences and work towards resolving emotional pain.

Chapter 10

REFLECTING AND MOVING FORWARD

Once you have come to recognize that you are avoidantly attached to people, what caused the problem, and how to start moving to a more secure attachment, you can start moving forward. It will probably be a lifelong journey because habits are hard to break, and there will be times when you will want to revert back to your avoidant behavior, especially in the early days. Even a decade later, you may find yourself falling back on the old ways of thinking. When you experience a major setback or relationship breakdown, you will definitely feel a strong desire to return to the attachment style. This is because you feel that it was justified.

It's not going to be smooth sailing, but you will find that your life is much more likely to improve over time. Especially as you build better connections with a wider network.

Reflecting on the Journey: From Avoidance to Security

When you first start the journey, you should be journaling about it. This should reflect your thoughts, feelings, and goals. And you should always have goals, even years after you feel that you have successfully changed your attachment style.

Periodically, you can return to this journal to reflect on how far you've come. This could mean establishing a healthy romantic relationship, better relationships with family, or even creating a closer friend group. It's a good idea to take the time to reflect because it reminds you of how your life has changed for the better. Sure there will be times when things

are rough, but you will have people who are willing to help you instead of trying to do it on your own.

The Quest for Independence and Self-Sufficiency

The way you view independence and self-sufficiency has almost certainly changed over time. It's no longer about being able to do everything for yourself, but being your own individual person within your community. You don't have to be an island to be successful – in fact in most cases, you need to be a part of a community to find success. This means that your question for independence and self-sufficiency has changed. Ironically, it probably means that you have a better understanding of what it is to be independent and self-sufficient as you relate it to how you interact with others. It's not about not needing other people, but being connected in a way that enhances who you are as an individual.

The Pursuit of Perfection and the Reality of Imperfection in Partnerships

Since you probably were looking for "the one" or "perfection" within your relationship for a long time, it can be difficult to accept that this isn't the goal. Mostly because it is entirely unrealistic. All relationships have give and take in them, and you should be doing both to make your partner happy. Your partner should be equally interested in seeking your happiness. Neither of you should be doing the majority of the work in the relationship, and that definitely includes the emotional aspect of the relationship.

Relationships will always be work, and a good partnership is even more work. It will never be perfect. And if it were, that would be incredibly boring. It's about finding someone who is right *for you* and someone you can work with to develop a strong attachment and good life.

You should stop seeking a perfect relationship, and focus on a relationship that is perfect for the life you want, with the understanding that you will need to work toward that goal together.

Exercise: Write a Reflective Piece on Your Journey from Avoidance to Security

Objective:

This exercise is designed to help you articulate and reflect on your personal journey from an avoidant attachment style towards a more secure attachment. Recognizing and appreciating your progress can reinforce your commitment to ongoing growth.

Instructions:

Step 1: Reflect on Your Starting Point

Think back to when you first recognized your avoidant attachment tendencies. Describe how this affected your relationships and your initial feelings about changing these patterns.

*Sta*_____

_____

_____

_____

_____

___

Step 2: Acknowledge Key Milestones and Challenges

Identify significant milestones you've achieved on your journey towards security, as well as any challenges you faced. Reflect on how you overcame these challenges or how they contributed to your growth.

Key Milestones and Challenges:

_____

_____

_____

_____

_____

Step 3: Evaluate Your Current State and Future Goals

Consider where you stand now in your journey towards secure attachment. Reflect on the changes you've noticed in yourself and your relationships. Outline future goals for continuing this journey.

Current State and Future Goals:

_____

_____

_____

_____

Outcome:

By writing this reflective piece, you aim to gain deeper insight into your personal growth journey, acknowledging how far you've come and where you still wish to go. This reflection can serve as both a testament to your progress and a roadmap for future development.

Exercise: Identify Areas of Personal and Relational Growth You Wish to Focus on Next

Objective:

This exercise encourages you to identify specific areas in your personal development and relationships where you wish to focus your growth efforts next. Setting targeted goals can help direct your energy and resources effectively.

Instructions:

Step 1: Assess Personal Growth Areas

Reflect on aspects of your personal development that you feel could benefit from further attention. This might include emotional regulation, self-esteem, or independence within interdependence.

Personal Growth Areas:

_____

_____

_____

_____

Step 2: Consider Relational Growth Opportunities

Think about your relationships and identify areas where you'd like to see improvement or deepen connections. This could relate to communication, vulnerability, or shared activities.

Relational Growth Opportunities:

_____

_____

_____

_____

_____

Step 3: Set Specific Goals

For each area identified in steps 1 and 2, set specific, achievable goals. Consider actions you can take to work towards these goals and how you will measure progress.

Specific Goals and Actions:

_____

_____

_____

_____

_____

Outcome:

Completing this exercise helps clarify your priorities for personal and relational growth, setting the stage for targeted efforts towards improving your well-being and the quality of your relationships. By focusing on specific areas, you can make more meaningful progress on your journey towards secure attachment and enriched connections.

Practical Exercise: Plan a Conversation About Your Attachment Journey with a Partner or Close Friend

Objective:

This exercise aims to deepen your connections by sharing your journey toward secure attachment with someone close to you. Opening up about your experiences and growth can enhance understanding and intimacy in your relationships.

Instructions:

1. **Select the Right Person and Setting:** Choose a partner or close friend you trust and feel comfortable with to share your journey. Plan to have this conversation in a quiet, private setting where you can speak openly without interruptions.
2. **Prepare Your Thoughts:** Before the conversation, take some time to reflect on your attachment journey—where you started, the progress you've made, and where you hope to go. Think about how this journey has impacted your relationship with them.
3. **Engage in the Conversation:** Share your reflections with your chosen person. Be open about your challenges, achievements, and the insights you've gained. Encourage them to ask questions and share their thoughts and feelings in response.

Outcome:

By sharing your attachment journey, this exercise fosters deeper emotional connections and mutual understanding with someone important in your life. It's an opportunity to celebrate your growth and discuss how you can support each other moving forward.

Practical Exercise: Commit to a New Habit That Promotes Relational or Personal Growth and Track Your Progress

Objective:

To foster continuous personal and relational growth by introducing and maintaining a new positive habit. Tracking your progress will help you stay committed and see the tangible benefits of your efforts.

Instructions:

1. **Choose a New Habit:** Select a habit that contributes to your personal or relational growth. This could be anything from daily mindfulness practice, regular exercise, setting aside time for deep conversations with loved ones, or practicing gratitude.

2. **Implement the Habit:** Start incorporating this habit into your daily routine. Set a specific time and context for this activity to help integrate it into your life more smoothly.

3. **Track Your Progress:** Keep a journal or log to track your adherence to this new habit and note any changes or improvements you observe in your personal well-being or relationships. Reflect on these observations weekly to assess the impact of your efforts.

Outcome:

This exercise is designed to support your ongoing journey of self-improvement and relational enhancement. By committing to a new habit and tracking your progress, you can see the positive effects of consistent effort over time, encouraging further growth and development.

CONCLUSION

Having made it this far, you have already started to learn to heal the emotional wounds that caused you to develop an avoidant attachment style. Yes, there are things you will need to do every day, but you've already learned what you need to know and what you can do to start managing your emotions and connections – instead of ignoring and avoiding them. Now it is time to start reflecting on your journey and planning to improve the quality of your life.

Self-reflection is going to be critical in their journey because that is the only way to really see how the changes you are making are starting to alter the way you react and think. Self-reflection is something that people need to practice far more often. The more self-aware you are, the better you will be able to counter your flight reflex and anxiety around making more secure attachments. Over time, you'll learn who you can trust, and you'll see that it can be far better than being alone.

Hopefully, you've found some ideas and exercises in this book that really resonated with you. When you started, you probably had a preconceived notion that changed while you read the book. If you started doing the exercises, this likely showed you how to start managing your emotions, coping with stress, and building better relationships.

Going forward, continue to practice these exercises, even once you feel that you have achieved everything you wanted to get from this book. Like learning a language, self-growth and self-discovery doesn't end during your lifetime. The person you will be in 10 years from now is different from who you will be 20 years from now, but those changes don't have to be extreme. Ongoing self-discovery and growth will make the journey much more enjoyable and rewarding. If you develop a habit of completing them regularly, you will be much better equipped to handle trouble in relationships without simply dropping those relationships.

As you continue to age, who you are will also shift and change. There will always be something new to discover about yourself, and that can help you to better communicate with others, as well as making you feel more positive about the world around you. This is a journey that you can take and enjoy for the rest of your life.

Made in the USA
Monee, IL
21 November 2024

70772615R00066